RIDING
DENVER'S RAILS

RIDING
DENVER'S RAILS

A MILE HIGH STREETCAR HISTORY

KEVIN PHARRIS

FOREWORD BY KENTON FORREST

Charleston   London

THE
History
PRESS

Published by The History Press
Charleston, SC 29403
www.historypress.net

Front Cover: Though the anthropomorphized streetcar on the sign was crying, the driver was all smiles as he made his last runs using the rails. Perhaps he, as with many Denver commuters, was looking forward to the shining era promised by buses. *RTD.*

Back Cover: Too young to understand the importance of the sign just behind her, a final streetcar ride is greeted with joy by a young Denver girl. Where might this day have taken her?

First published 2013

Manufactured in the United States

ISBN 978.1.60949.915.0

Library of Congress CIP data applied for.

CONTENTS

FOREWORD

My family left Minnesota in 1955 for Denver, a city that had been entirely shaped by the streetcar and its predecessors. All the same, by the time we arrived, almost all of it was gone. Tracks were being paved over, the overhead wires were being taken down and the streetcars and trolley coaches that had once connected to those wires were being dismantled and discarded. To be certain, there were transit vehicles still on the streets, but a story stretching back more than eighty years had ended. Denver was moving resolutely into the future.

The diesel-powered buses rolling along Denver's streets still fascinated me, and once I began examining more closely, I realized that they connected to a lost world of transit. I was captivated, and a passion for Denver's transit began, growing throughout my entire life, a passion that has fueled almost every non-working moment. How did the trolley cars get from one end of the line to the other? Why did the routes change, and how? Who were the people, and what were their stories? The tramway is getting further and further away from us now, but it remains a very real element of the present for those of who have made its study our life's work.

This book is not meant to be the definitive, all-inclusive source on Denver's transit history. Those books have already been written as the three-volume work known as *Denver's Street Railways*, a portion of which I wrote and edited. Rather, this book is intended to introduce a new generation of Denverites to something that, even today, is dramatically affecting our city.

The first chapter provides a brief overview, drawn from numerous sources, of the region's rich transit history. Denver is not the only city in the United States that expanded because of transit, but we cannot study them all in one short book. Through extrapolation, and allowing for some local variations, we may understand the general course of transit in the United States from the earliest omnibuses to the modern fleet of buses ubiquitous in many urban American cities.

Streetcars last worked the rails of Denver in 1950, so more than sixty years divide us from their era. The ever-increasing amount of time is steadily robbing us of the voices who can speak to us about the experience of riding the streetcar. I have had the honor to work with some of the great figures in transit history and have experienced the grief of seeing us lose these invaluable founts of information. The personal recollections of members of the general public have no less impact, however, and these voices are also being lost. The second chapter of this book focuses on their stories and impressions, lending an individual connection undimmed by the numerous decades. The author has asked to include my own story, and it is contained there as well.

Chapter three examines the modern day and the return of multi-modal transit to Denver and the region. I am glad Denver is moving ahead with these projects, because those of us who call the city home will be well-served by the sound planning and decisions that are now building infrastructure for the future. It will not be built in a day, but neither were the original streetcar lines and the cities they served.

It is vital that we continue studying the history of transit in Denver, keep reading about it and keep writing about it. In doing so, we will all come to understand that we are not creating something new on the ashes of everything that came before us. We are continuing their inspired work, and what a ride it will be. All aboard!

Kenton Forrest

ACKNOWLEDGEMENTS

This book is dedicated to Shawn Snow. His passion for history in general and transit in specific enriches us all!

This book would not have been possible without the generosity of those who shared their memories, pictures, information and time, especially Kenton Forrest, the folks at the Colorado Railroad Museum, the Denver Tramway Heritage Society and the Regional Transportation District. Thank you!

Many pictures in this volume may be attributed to the following: the Denver Municipal Facts (DMF); the Denver Tramway Heritage Society (DTHS); the Colorado Railroad Museum (CRM); the Regional Transportation District (RTD); and the Englewood Public Library (EPL). Those not otherwise accredited are in the author's personal collection.

CHAPTER 1

THE TICKET TO THE FUTURE

Denver once had an extensive system of electrically powered transit, composed of more than 250 miles of track within the Denver metropolitan area and 40 miles of high-speed interurban rail, connecting the city with Golden and Boulder. For work, shopping, school and entertainment, Denver's streetcars were a fully integrated part of daily life. Despite this, all streetcar service was abandoned in 1950. In the first chapter of *Riding Denver's Rails*, we examine the history, in Denver and otherwise, that led to the streetcar's meteoric rise and equally dramatic fall, all within less than a full century.

Even as this book is being written, transit is being hotly discussed in and around Denver. One of the discussions focuses on a new campaign put out by the Denver Regional Council of Governments (known as DRCOG), which includes billboards, advertisements on the sides of buses and Light Rail trains, as well as radio promotions and an explanatory website. The website lists ways to avoid being an "SOV," which is a transit acronym for "single occupancy vehicle." According to the website, one may carpool, vanpool, bike, work from home, use park and rides (to get to work via bus or train) or walk. The intention is to decrease the number of trips with a single person in the car—about 75 percent of all outings in the metropolitan area. As the city continues to grow—and in anticipation of putting more cars on the road—the proposal makes sense.

Owing to the perhaps not-so-accidental similarity the acronym has to a more offensive one, the advertising campaign has garnered some criticism.

Hudson invades, indeed! The year 1950 would see the streetcars leave Denver for good, replaced by the automobile as the preferred mode of transit. *RTD.*

Advertising on public transit vehicles is nothing new. Long before today's buses were emblazoned, Denver's streetcars played host to messages that reflected the times. Though this document was issued in 1968, the image from the past is still eloquent in its reminder.

Bob Whitson, executive director of Boulder Transportation Connections, agreed with the goal of getting more people to explore transit options but felt the campaign was "negative and anti-car." The *Denver Post* called the ads "cheeky." The communications and marketing director at DRCOG, Steve Erickson, countered that the ads were meant to be playful.

Whether cheeky or playful and whether successful in reducing the number of single-person trips in and around Denver, the discussion is emblematic of a larger theme: once transportation methods other than walking developed, there have been debates, sometimes exceedingly acrimonious, about the right way to get around and especially who would pay for such services. The debate is likely to continue no matter what new technologies lie in the future.

Even in the distant past, transit improvements were a ticket to the future: signs of civilization and all that went with it. For example, the Romans were famous for their roads, which moved troops quickly and facilitated commerce, intellectual exchange and a broader sense of place.

Before Europeans colonized North America, the Native Americans traveled and traded in generally well-established spheres and along well-understood routes, most often the many rivers of the continent's interior. Colonizing of the continent began on its eastern fringe, which, by default, led most transportation seekers to the sea. With westward expansion, the same watery highways served European settlers. As communities grew in size and distance from those around them, the similarities to European transit began to end. In the book *Economic Transformation of America: 1600 to Present*, Robert Heilbroner illustrates the difference between what had been familiar and practical in Europe and the extreme challenges presented on the North American continent.

> One of [the serious problems] *was the marked isolation of the average American establishment. In England, thanks to the smallness of the nation and to its peculiarly indented coast, a network of transportation bound the parts of the country into a more or less unified market. With no town more than seventy miles from the sea and with at least 20,000 miles of turnpike-highway (much of it admittedly execrable), England was knit together into an economic whole.*

This "economic whole" in England contrasts with an American model of transit difficulties. During the War of 1812, with American access to coastal traffic cut off, "it cost more to drag a ton of iron ten miles through the Pennsylvania hills than to bring it across the ocean, and the inland freight on corn was so high it was unmarketable outside a radius of a few miles from its origin." Canals, tolled turnpikes and steamboats were the earliest attempts to address this dearth of transit options.

The famous Erie Canal opened in 1825, an engineering marvel connecting Lake Erie and the Hudson River. For a while, canals seemed to be the country's future, but their successors were fast approaching. The first steam railway operated in the United States in 1828, the same year as the first major gold rush in the country, which would lure many to northern Georgia and lead to the founding of the original city of Auraria. By the 1840s, railroads were ending the halcyon days of canal travel and making some people very rich. Railroads, however, worked best over long distances. They were not suited to visiting one's relatives across town. Within one's daily life, transit still depended on the forms of movement dominant for millennia: walking, riding horses and using horse-drawn conveyances.

However charming an image one might have of riding a horse about town, the realities are far less romantic. As cities grew, feeding and stabling became problems. In the 1860s, New York City had over 1,000,000 people in the metropolitan area. Philadelphia had over 560,000, and six other American cities (Baltimore, Boston, New Orleans, Cincinnati, St. Louis and Chicago) each contained more than 100,000. If each person had a horse, the stabling alone would have been enormous. Consider, as well, the other "contribution" from horses. In New York's Central Park in the early part of this decade, where carriage horses took park visitors on scenic rides through this oasis of green in the bustling metropolis, each horse produced about ten pounds of manure per day. So around seventy horses serving the park produced nearly seven hundred pounds. This manure needed to be gathered and disposed of or it became a nuisance. City residents who used the park encountered much being missed.

Extrapolate this outward, then, to a time when horses were more numerous. In 1900, the city of Rochester, New York, estimated its horse population to be about fifteen thousand. In one year, those animals produced enough manure to create a pile that would cover an entire acre to a depth of over 150 feet. In the words of Professor Joel Tarr, of Carnegie-Mellon University, an expert in urban development in the United States during the early 1900s, "The old gray mare was not the ecological marvel, in American cities, that horse lovers like to believe." Manure powdered when trampled or driven on and became a dust that covered neighborhoods (and food) in times of dry weather. (This lack of excrement would one day be cited as one of the benefits of automobiles, though the exhaust created by gasoline and diesel-powered vehicles may well render that belief null.) As the populations of American cities continued to grow, another answer was clearly necessary.

Though it was the twenty-fifth-largest city in the nation as the 1900s dawned, a mere forty-two years earlier, no one would have guessed what was to come for Denver. The interior of the continent had long held little interest for most of the voyagers from the eastern United States. It had been labeled the "Great American Desert" for decades, a misnomer that would dissuade permanent settlement, even when people traveling through found direct and contradictory evidence in the surroundings. The alluring sirens of gold and land in Oregon and California would not be silenced, at least not until an equally loud siren let loose her voice along the front range of the Rocky Mountains. With the discovery of gold in the region, the Great American Desert was no longer as unappealing. Denver was founded toward the end of 1858 and would serve for years as the jumping-off point for people seeking instant riches. Within a decade, the Denver Horse Railroad Company was founded, and within a few more years, the first tracks were being laid. The company was given an exclusive franchise, which was intended to last thirty-five years.

The core of the city lay along Larimer Street, named for the founder of the city, William Larimer. The highest concentration of buildings stretched along Larimer from Cherry Creek to Twentieth Street. In the opposite direction, Fifteenth and Sixteenth Streets were the city's primary arteries, the city's core stretching from Wynkoop to Champa. In these areas and beyond, the city was stagnant in population growth. The first interstate train reached Denver in 1870, shortly after the Denver Horse Railroad Company had been founded. With it came more people and more investment. For visitors and locals alike, the distances necessary to walk were becoming cumbersome, and distance was only part of the problem. In the summer, roads were dusty. In periods of rain or snow, they became muddy quagmires. Though most people walked out of necessity, muddy roads could also play havoc with horseback riders and horse-drawn conveyances. The city needed a solution.

Fortunately, the first track put in by the Denver Horse Railroad Company began service on January 2, 1872. (Part of the delay in initiating horsecar service within the city was the wait to see if the train would actually reach Denver. With the Union Pacific going through Cheyenne and crossing Wyoming but not Denver, many believed the promising city in the region was our neighbor to the north. Many investors intentionally delayed. If Denver had not found a way to connect itself to the railroad in 1870, this book might well have been about Cheyenne instead.) The Denver Horse Railroad Company's inaugural line stretched from the heart of today's Auraria campus, then a bustling neighborhood known as West Denver, over Cherry Creek at Larimer to Sixteenth, where it turned southeast before turning northeast again and running along Champa to Twenty-eighth Street.

Champa Street, without much along it, might have seemed an odd choice to outfit with a mass transit offering. Denver's first public park, Curtis Park, had been donated to the city in 1868 and lay just beyond the end of the line. Also nearby was Billy Wise's National Park, which served good-quality liquors. Despite these draws, the choice seemed strange to many given that transit's main purpose is to transport people. A reporter for the *Rocky Mountain News*, commenting on the horsecar line leading into oblivion, declared the area "remote and unvaluable." Despite this, the reporter asserted that homes would surely sprout along the route, drawn thither by the nearby amenities and the possibility of getting in and out of downtown on the horsecar.

The reporter was right. When the train arrived in Denver, it brought an enormous increase in the city's population, and these folks needed to live somewhere. Before the decade was over, large brick homes were rising along the horsecar's length, conveying on Curtis Park, as it is known today, the honor of being Denver's first streetcar suburb. Other buildings, not just residences, would follow the horsecar line into the neighborhood. The city's first Temple Emanuel, at Nineteenth and Curtis (where the Ritz Carlton is today), would relocate into Curtis Park in 1882. Located at the corner of Twenty-fourth and Curtis, the building still stands today. It was a synagogue for the Temple Emanuel until 1899 and, afterward, the Beth HaMedrosh Hagodol congregation. Where people went, so went the institutions to serve them. Whether for pleasure, prayer or personal space, the horsecar got people there.

This pattern would repeat itself again and again in Denver, with transit providing ease and access for the growth of neighborhoods. Supplying transit for Denver's burgeoning population was a financial lure as well. Lewis Ellsworth, who reached Denver in 1871, came in representation of investors from Chicago. Whether he came specifically to invest in transit or not is unknown, but it evidently proved tempting enough. Ellsworth and his colleagues bought the original franchise and put in the tracks to Curtis Park. Expansions would follow, and Ellsworth is honored for his part in developing early Denver with a street name. Ellsworth Avenue is the 000 block, dividing south Denver from north Denver. Though this degree of tribute is unintentional, as the numbering system would come later, the

Downtown Denver was not the only place benefiting from the presence of the streetcar. Neighborhood streetcars allowed most homes access to lines just outside their front doors or a short walk away. *CRM.*

veneration is likely deserved, for transit would completely determine how the city would grow for almost eighty years.

The years that followed involved some name changes for the company, and its venture was a profitable one for the owners. It was not hugely profitable, however, for much of the money earned in public transit would flow back into the system. Maintaining track, vehicles and animals and paying staff were only part of the cost. As the city grew, so grew demand for more and more transit lines to be opened. The cost of extensions and new lines prevented the dividends from being particularly large. Nevertheless, the Denver City Railway Company, as it was now known, kept building. The name change, in the words of Kevin Flynn at the Regional Transportation District (RTD), occurred because the company had made its first foray into "multi-modal" transit. In addition to using horses to provide power, the company had bought some mules.

Public transit required the creation of new forms of etiquette. One enterprising young man in Denver, the *Rocky Mountain News* reported, in riding the horsecars to observe his fellow passengers, noted that one in ten men left the car without paying his fare. Gentlemen were usually willing to give their seats to a lady, especially when the cars were crowded. This was the obligation of any well-bred man, for women were "less fitted for such hardships and annoyances," like standing in a moving vehicle. Men were obliged to help women from the car at a stop. Also, men should not extend their legs into the walkway of the carriage, as this would trip people. These expressions of decorous behavior were being played out all over the nation. Almost every major city in the country busily spread its transit webs. With plenty of land to spread into, Denver was never compelled to go underground for its transit needs. That would have been prohibitively expensive. The eyes in Denver's downtown were turned outward with plans for unstopped growth.

One of the big questions on everyone's minds: where would Mr. Ellsworth and the company expand next? The simple answer was almost everywhere. By 1881, new horsecar lines had opened along Park Avenue, south on Broadway and along Welton. The original lines on Larimer and Champa were also expanded. These lines illustrate the general trend of the city's growth, toward the northeast and the Curtis Park, Five Points and Whittier neighborhoods (drawing its name from an elementary school in the area honoring well-known abolitionist John Greenleaf Whittier) and toward the southeast, where the first mansions of Capitol Hill were already enjoying their unimpeded view of the Rocky Mountains on the western horizon.

A general growth to the east seemed sensible. There were no significant topographical barriers in that direction. It is curious, then, that Lewis Ellsworth chose the northwest for a major transit expansion. Though the South Platte River had been derided by Mark Twain and many others as nothing of import, it would still present a more demanding barrier. Moreover, to the west of the river were high bluffs, the reason for the area's first name: Highland. How would the horsecars scale the river and then ascend the steep angle to the land above the river? The challenges would be overcome, if sufficient reason could be found to justify it. The reason for Ellsworth's choice may well lie in the fact that two gentlemen, John Clough and W.G. Sprague, were erecting a new two-story hotel in the area, at the corner of Seventeenth Avenue and what is today Federal Boulevard. Clough was the secretary for the Denver City Railway Company. According to the authors of *Denver's Street Railways*, "he no doubt exerted some influence on securing public transportation for his new enterprise, the Grand View House."

The Grand View, sometimes referred to as "hotel," drew larger crowds on Sundays, many of them ruffians and thugs who "smoke in the cars and sometimes use coarse and ungentlemanly language, but that class can't be decent anywhere." The observer of streetcar behavior continued, saying, "In making nine trips over the various lines, [I] saw only two drunken men

A picture postcard sent in 1921 to Miss M.J. Alexander, R.D. #9, Penn Yan, New York. "Dear sister. A line to let you know I received your and Mom's welcome letter this morning with enclosure. Glad to know your colds are getting better. Love to all, Calvin." The capitol and the spires of Immaculate Conception would be recognizable for Denverites of today. Missing in the foreground is the curve at the northern edge of Civic Center Park as well as the building that curve now accommodates, the Voorhies Memorial.

on the cars. One of those was inclined to be noisy and stared at ladies rather insultingly. The other was stupidly drunk and curled down in the corner by the door, and went to sleep." This mixing of people of various classes and comportments would, one day, be one of the main reasons people found the automobile so appealing.

So it went in Denver, with the mad pace of transit expansion showing little sign of abating. The Woeber Brothers Carriage Company, which had a plant at Eleventh Street and Walnut (today an athletic field on the Auraria Campus), began producing horsecars for the company in 1884. Their cars would serve in cities across the West, from Salt Lake City, Utah, and Butte, Montana, to Trinidad, Colorado, and Salina, Kansas. From 1898 until 1913, the Woeber Brothers Carriage Company built most of the cars owned by the Denver Tramway.

The Denver Tramway Company is a name that would come to have a long association with Denver's transportation, both in the past and today, but it was not the first competitor to threaten the Denver City Railway Company. One early entrant into the hodgepodge of companies that would one day litter the Denver landscape was the Denver Circle Railroad,

Placed by the streetcar's manufacturers, the plaque rests in Car 610, one of the last vehicles built for the Denver Tramway by the Woeber Brothers.

created by William A.H. Loveland. A powerful figure in the early history of the territory and state, Loveland was a proponent of Golden to serve as capital. Though this proposition failed to bear fruit, other diverse efforts, from railroads to agriculture to education, were successful. In Denver, he was the main force behind the Denver Circle Line, as it was also commonly known, which ran south to the area around today's Overland Park as well as southwest toward today's Valverde neighborhood, a separate city from 1888 until 1902. Loveland anticipated that the line would stimulate residential growth to the south of Denver, which proved to be true, another example of the growth in Denver following transit opportunities. An additional draw to the southern extent of Denver was the National Mining Exposition, which was so popular that it lasted longer than the one year intended. After it completed its 1882–1885 run, Baron von Richtofen took over the location for his Sans Souci Beer Garden. Commuter traffic along the Denver Circle Line increased as prairie land was converted into homes and people came to fill them. Later residents, dependent on transit to reach downtown

Denver, would press for continued service as transportation companies and methods developed.

The all-important element of transit would make or break many real estate ventures. The authors of *Denver Street Railways* explain it thusly:

> *Today, when a residential neighborhood or a new shopping center complex is developed, the developers themselves make sure their project is located close to an arterial highway, or, if it is not, they endeavor to persuade governmental authorities to undertake such highway development. In 1885, by contrast, very few people could afford a private conveyance, and even the affluent often preferred to leave their carriages at home and use public transportation. Thus, business and residential real estate development hinged upon proximity to a street railway line. If one was nearby, well and good. If not, developers would either build their own street-railway line or persuade the management of the existing streetcar company to extend a route to the site of the new promotion.*

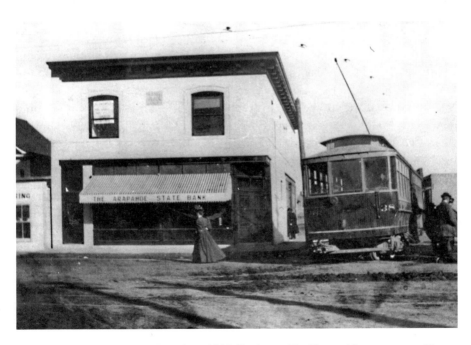

As seen in this photograph taken about 1910, Englewood had been able to grow steadily owing to its active connection to downtown Denver. The streetcars served reliably and regularly except for the early morning hours, when it was assumed everyone would be asleep. *EPL.*

Andrew Carnegie would have understood this process, having stated, "90 percent of all millionaires became so through real estate." In Denver, real-estate wealth depended on transportation.

In 1885, the number of companies promoters could court added a new player. In that year, the Denver Electric and Cable Company incorporated, obtaining a charter from the city to use its streets. The fare was limited to five cents. The following year, in 1886, the company merged with another entity, the Denver Railway Association, to form the Denver Tramway Company. Some of the biggest names in the city's early history were involved with this entity: former territorial governor John Evans; his son, William Gray Evans; William Newton Byers, of the *Rocky Mountain News*; and Henry Cordes Brown, the mogul behind Capitol Hill's development and the eventual construction of today's Brown Palace Hotel.

These men and their associates got around the exclusive franchise awarded to the original Denver Horse Railroad Company by using a new technology: cars moved by running cables. The same technology still operates the famous cable cars in San Francisco today. The Denver Tramway Company built a large powerhouse at the southwest corner of Colfax and Broadway, in what is today Civic Center Park. The original lines ran east along Colfax, south along Broadway and northwest along Fifteenth Street. The company would eventually have nearly 160 miles of track and a fleet of 250 cars, but in the beginning, it was merely another actor on the scene.

The company's choice of "tramway" for its name has created some confusion for Denver's transit historians. This is a British term. Though the word was used throughout the British Empire and in a number of non-British countries that had paid for their transit systems with British financing, this was not how Americans referred to their city transit providers. American companies were "railroads," "railways" or "traction" companies. Within the United States, the Denver Tramway Company was almost unique in its choice of names, and the basis for picking "tramway" remains unknown.

Cable cars, invented in San Francisco in 1873, were put to use in a number of American cities. They were faster than horses, did not become sick or fatigued and ran obligingly as long as power was maintained. Denver had a ready source of coal from intrastate markets. The only difficulties lay in digging the coal out and getting it to Denver. A growing population and abundant inflow of immigrant labor into the United States answered those needs, so the Denver Tramway Company's power requirements would only be interrupted through unusual circumstances, as we will see later.

A picture postcard, posted in 1908, shows two of Denver's fine hotels. Unlike the Brown Palace Hotel, at left, the Savoy would be torn down for the construction of a skyscraper. The postcard was sent to Mr. E. Murray, of Rensselaer Falls, New York. "Hello Elom, how are you? I thought I would send you a card and tell you I had watermelon Sunday for dinner. Come out and have some. John." The car shown is a Seeing Denver Car, an easy way for tourists to get around in the day.

Today, the Byers-Evans House serves as a museum, linking visitors to one of the most powerful figures in the tramway's history, William Gray Evans. Though not visible at this distance, the window to the left of the front door bears a mark of the 1920 strike, when someone fired a gun at the house.

The skyscrapers of downtown are not yet in evidence in this shot looking northwest across Broadway. Where the sign reads, "Country Club Beer," the offices of the Denver Post stand today. Directly behind the streetcar, hidden by its form, is the Pioneer Monument, and the vehicles passing each other to the right of the streetcar are east and westbound on Colfax.

Looking northwest on Fifteenth Street, the dearth of tall buildings is a stark difference in this scene from June 1950. The grassy area to the left of the streetcar is the northern expanse of Civic Center Park.

Built on the site of his father's home, William Gray Evans had the tramway building erected to serve as offices, a car barn and a support facility for the many staff members of Denver's only transit provider. Today, the beautiful building has been lovingly restored and serves as the Hotel Teatro.

The Denver City Railway Company originally saw the Denver Tramway Company as just another upstart, surely destined to succumb to the vagaries of a demanding transit situation in Denver. The Denver City Railway Company continued to build aggressively, expanding and updating its animal-drawn service. By 1887, under thirty years from the founding of the city, the company had thirty miles of track, and almost every area of the city was within a few blocks of a horsecar line. The company boasted eighty horsecars, more than one hundred drivers and numerous horses that kept the cars running at ten-minute intervals from six in the morning until midnight, an astounding depth and breadth of service considering the amount of time the company had been serving.

The cars themselves were improving as well, including small touches that sometimes created large reactions, as pointed out in *Denver's Street Railways* with some amusement. "Another feature, and one that strikes the passengers with astonishment, is a looking-glass directly above the cash box, so located that the passenger paying his fare can see if his mustache is blooming." Local judge Amos Steck declared it would save money for male travelers. "No lady will allow a gentleman to pay her fare when, by paying it herself, she can ascertain if her bonnet is on straight."

As the 1880s were drawing to a close, Denver's real estate market was ballooning outward, making many investors and companies a great deal of money. This promising market attracted attention from financiers beyond the city limits. In order to capitalize on the trend, these investors would frequently buy huge tracts of land outside the city limits as well, in hopes of luring development to those parts of the region. These companies often built their own railways to serve their nascent communities. One of the first of these distant communities was Montclair, platted in 1885. The Colfax Avenue Railway was incorporated in 1887 to carry people to and from Montclair, the railway shifting to steam in 1888. *Denver's Street Railways* described the primary concern that might impede Montclair's success: "Buyers could be attracted [to the Montclair development] only if they could be convinced that there would be convenient transportation between their new homes and the teeming mart of commerce Denver was rapidly becoming."

Arapahoe County, which stretched east of Denver's city limits at York Street, had given the Colfax Avenue Railway the right to operate along the thoroughfare. The company's efforts did not proceed without some barriers in its path, however; at first neither the Denver Tramway nor the Denver City Railway were willing to build east far enough to connect to the line terminating at York Street, effectively cutting Montclair and all eastern

The chimney bears the words "Loop Market." The streetcar in the foreground is similarly labeled, helping users navigate Denver's transit system. The entrance is in the front, the exit farther back. Riders paid as they entered. For interurban cars, riders paid as they left.

locales off from Denver. After some histrionics and permutations, the Denver City Railway would eventually complete the link that was lacking.

Those real estate ventures that could not quite afford to build their own transit systems would offer money to the extant companies in hopes of luring their service. By the end of 1888, the first cable lines were in operation. Cable and horse cars allowed men of ordinary means to maintain a residence outside the expensive heart of the city while still having access for work and entertainment. The *Denver Times* reported that "the effect upon suburban property will swell the volume of real estate transactions for a long time to come." All the newspapers of the day bore out these assertions. Advertisers touted new properties located along streetcar lines, especially to the northwest of the city. Berkeley showed itself especially popular, in part owing to the number of nearby pleasure retreats: Berkeley Lake, Rocky Mountain Lake and Elitch Gardens. The Berkeley Park Rapid Transit served to take people not only to and from work but also to and from these venues. Berkeley's population grew steadily, which no doubt pleased those who had invested in it as a profit-making venture. This, in turn, spurred the hopes of real estate fortunes in others. The competition to attract the all-important streetcar would be intense.

DENVER DAILY DOINGS   17

SHORT STREET CAR RIDES

BERKELEY PARK.—Tennis courts and free bathing beach. A delightful spot in which to picnic. Take Route 7 or 8 cars northbound on 16th street.

CITY PARK.—The largest of the city parks. Has municipal golf links, zoo, electric fountain, tennis courts, conservatory, two lakes, and boating. Reached by Route 40 car on 17th street.

WASHINGTON PARK.—The second largest in the city, and is known as one of the most beautifully laid out of its kind in the country. Boating, tennis and free municipal bathing beach. Reached by Route 29 car southbound on 15th street or Route 58 car on 18th street.

CHEESMAN PARK.—From the Cheesman Memorial, located in the Park, there is an unobstructed view of over 100 miles of mountain range. Take Route 13 car on 17th street and alight at Gilpin street.

ELITCH'S GARDENS.—Famous throughout the country for their home-like restfulness. In the little theater, almost every theatrical star of renown has played, and scores have made their debut in this quiet spot. You have not seen Denver until you have spent a half hour in the bower of the Gardens. Take Route 7 or 8 car northbound on 16th street, or Route 38 at the Central Loop.

LAKESIDE.—The big million-dollar amusement park of Denver. There are over forty distinct Coney Island attractions in the park, including the finest bathing beach in Denver. All tourists who break their journey at Denver take a trip to Lakeside to spend an hour or two enjoying the fun-making devices. Take Route 7 or 8 car northbound on 16th street.

STATE CAPITOL AND STATE MUSEUM.—Located at Colfax avenue and Sherman street. The State Museum, which is just across the street from the capitol on Sherman street, contains a very fascinating exhibit of historical interest. All the relics of the stirring pioneer days of Colorado; of the Indian Wars; of the Civil War; mummies and remains of the Cliff Dwellers of Colorado; skulls of the fanatical Flat-Head Indians; basket-weaving exhibits and ancient implements of warfare, are gathered here. They include hundreds of individual trophies, such as Kit Carson's rifle with its twenty-nine brass tacks—"Every tack a dead Indian." Take Route 10 car on 15th street, or Route 13 car on 17th street.

CITY PARK MUSEUM.—Reached by Route 40 car on 17th street. The view of the mountain range from in front of the museum is one you

will never forget. On the first and second floors of the museum are mounted animal exhibits which have made it famous everywhere. The animals are grouped naturally in reproductions of their habitat which are marvelously accurate and really beautiful. No brief word description of these exhibits of buffalo, deer, mountain sheep, mountain lions, musk ox, grizzlies, beavers and birds can make you realize the wonder of the collection. Other exhibits include live reptiles and fish. On the second floor is the art gallery and the well known Denver collection of ancient Chinese and Japanese pottery and carvings. In the basement among hundreds of other exhibits will be found the Safe of Gold, probably the

BATHING BEACH AT WASHINGTON PARK

world's only exhibit of solid crystallized gold just as it comes from the mines; the diamond drill core from a bore hole 2,006 feet deep through the earth's crust of the La Platte River; the head and jaws of a huge monster that lived in the fresh water lakes that covered the land from Colorado Springs to Montana; the radium exhibit; the reproduction of the beautiful white grotto of the Grand Cavern in Old Mexico and pieces of stars that have fallen to earth.

GOLDEN.—The first capitol of Colorado, located in the foothills just 14 miles from Denver. The main gateway to Denver's Municipal Parks and Lookout Mountain. One of the shortest but most beautiful trips around Denver. Half hourly service from the Interurban Loop, located on Arapahoe street between 14th and 15th streets.

TO LOCATE DENVER ADVERTISERS, USE MAP ON PAGE 6

In *Denver Daily Doings*, published in 1925, visitors to the city could learn about all the essentials for getting the most out of a visit to Denver. One of the most essential was listing all of the amenities within an easy streetcar ride. Colorful language was the standard for the day!

While these competing companies were testing each other's mettle—building lines served by animals, cables and steam—events were taking place far to the east of Denver that would forever change the city's transit face. These changes would not be limited to Denver; indeed, a simple change in technology, successfully tested and then applied in Richmond, Virginia, would sweep across the nation like a storm, and no city's transit package would be the same afterward.

Attempts to refine the basic technologies around transit had been ongoing. Tinkerers would propose many modifications, most of which were minor, a few of which were game altering. Sidney Short, from the University of Denver, would invent the first electrified transit method attempted in Denver. Short designed a system built around an electrified third rail. Although this seemed a likely success when tested, it failed to fulfill its promise when in actual use on the street. Though ostensibly shielded from casual contact with people and animals above it, the third rail had a nasty tendency to shock passersby when water was present. Not life-threatening to people making contact between the electrified rail and those that bore no current, it was alarming and slightly painful. More problematic was when horses made the connection. Startled animals would tear through the streets, endangering their riders and everyone else in their frenzied, pell-mell course. Though still used in some subways today, such as those beneath New York City, the electrified rail system would last for only a small time in Denver.

Some transit-oriented inventors, however, enjoyed phenomenal success. Frank Julien Sprague pioneered the streetcar powered by connecting to an overhead power source, a wire suspended between poles along the road's length. Though some feared the lines would fall during accidents or inclement weather, leading to electrocution, these fears were demonstrated to be baseless. Soon, Sprague's streetcars were being replicated across the nation, a technological leap that would be unassailable. In *Light Rail and Heavy Politics*, author Jack McCroskey draws some figures together to illustrate how Sprague's technology conquered the country. "In 1890, the first year the federal government took a transit census and two years after Sprague's success in Richmond, electric trolleys accounted for 1,200 miles of track or fifteen percent of the total. By 1902, the number had shot up to 25,000 miles or ninety-eight percent of the total—a stratospheric growth rate amounting to almost thirty percent a year for the entire twelve years."

This technology not yet having reached Denver, the city's transit companies continued blithely forward with the same modes they had been using. The companies eagerly built to any place that seemed to justify the presence of transit. Riverfront Park, created by John Brisbane Walker to be Denver's first amusement park, received an extension right to its front door in 1889. (Today's Commons Park sits on the site of the former amusement park, no traces left of its existence except in documents and photographs.) The Denver Tramway's cable lines reached all the way to the jewel of Denver: City Park. The cable car made a loop at Fillmore and Detroit at Seventeenth Avenue for the return trip to downtown Denver. There on Seventeenth Avenue, visitors would later disembark at the beautiful Sopris Gate, named for one of the fathers of the park. The Denver and Berkeley Park Rapid Transit line was incorporated in 1888 to serve the separate cities of Highlands and Berkeley, eventually allowing access to Elitch Gardens (1889) and the White City, as Lakeside Amusement Park (1908) was frequently known.

The array of competing companies would become dizzying: the Highlands Street Railroad, the Park Railway, the University Park Railway and Electric Company and the South Denver Cable Railway Company were some that sprang up in and around Denver. That same year, the Denver City Railway Company, the original service provider in Denver, renamed itself the Denver City Cable Railway Company, beginning a shift in its focus from animal-drawn cars to those that would be powered by moving cables.

Steadily, Denver neighborhoods took on some of the aspects that would serve as some of the most important legacies of the streetcars in our modern day. Where streetcars stopped it was certain that passengers would be getting off and on them. People congregating in an area means there will be money to spend, and businesses are sure to follow. Though most homes today have a refrigerator, allowing for infrequent shopping, the families of the late 1800s and early 1900s often shopped daily. Grocery stores and other businesses slated to meet daily needs were located within neighborhoods, a convenient walk away. Before heading home for the evening, commuters would often stop to pick up necessary supplies. By locating businesses together, they could sustain enough density to nourish them. Where streetcar stops coincided with major streets, denser business districts would spring up to serve the neighborhood. As Chapter Three will discuss, these pockets of retail density, such as that by the streetcar stop at the intersection of Thirty-second Avenue and Lowell, were the standard way for many Denverites to conduct their lives.

The Denver Circle Line had drawn enough people to settle the area south of Alameda that the separate city of South Denver, founded in 1886, was experiencing very satisfactory growth. The South Denver Cable Railway Company began offering electric trolley service to the area in 1889. Another growing subdivision south of South Denver, known then as Orchard Place,

The Sorpris Gate, named for one of the fathers of City Park, Richard Sopris, once served as the front door to City Park for those reaching this Denver jewel by streetcar. *DMF.*

Robbed of streetcar patrons, the Sopris Gate is today the least used of the four gateways into City Park. Driven by and jogged by, its isolation is a sad fall from the days when it would have served numerous revelers using the park.

The Denver City Cable Railway Company constructed this building as a power station at the corner of Eighteenth Street and Lawrence. The name for the originating company is still proudly emblazoned at the top of the building, though today it serves as the Old Spaghetti Factory.

Though the vehicle was not one belonging to the Denver City Cable Railway Company, the spirit is accurate. Visitors to the Old Spaghetti Factory today may enjoy their meals in an old streetcar outfitted with tables and chairs instead of the rattan seats and fare boxes of yesteryear.

The Goodheart Laundry Building still stands on South Broadway. The South Division Yards, where cars assembled in between runs, however, does not.

was the residential kernel that would eventually become Englewood. Horsecars and cable cars were extending the city in every direction, but horsecars were destined to have the shorter tenure.

In his work of fiction *Time and Again*, Jack Finney describes a young woman's journey from the modern day (1970, in this case) to New York City in 1882. The account illustrates how, though an advanced technology for the day, horsecars were still a gritty experience compared with what was to come:

> *It wasn't a good night for walking, and at Sixteenth Street I looked back over my shoulder, and a streetcar was trundling along toward me, the horse's head bent to the wind, the kerosene lanterns flickering at the front of the car. It stopped for me, I got on the front platform, and the horse leaned into his collar, his metal-shod hoofs slipping and sliding heavily in the snow till we got rolling along. Here on the open platform, where the driver could watch it, hung a fare box, and I dropped in my nickel, opened the door, and stepped in, closing the door against the wind. I walked down the aisle, crunching dirty wet straw under my feet, and sat down. The tin-shaded lamp hanging from the ceiling smoked badly, and the kerosene smell was very strong.*

Americans have always been interested in newer and better ways of doing things. In *At Home*, Bill Bryson discusses the Great Exposition of 1851, which took place in London. "[American oversights in preparing for the event] reinforced the more or less universal conviction that Americans were little more than amiable backwoodsmen not yet ready for unsupervised outings on the world stage. So it came as something of a surprise when the displays [at the exposition] were erected to discover that the American section was an outpost of wizardry and wonder. Nearly all the American machines did things that the world earnestly wished machines to do—stamp out nails, cut stone, mould candles—but with a neatness, dispatch and tireless reliability that left other nations blinking." Howe's sewing machine, McCormick's reaper and Colt's repeat-action revolver were, for many Europeans, some of "the first unsettling hint[s] that those tobacco-chewing rustics across the water were quietly creating the next industrial colossus." Americans have never been a people to settle for the old ways when there is a new way to get something done faster.

As a result, in 1889, Denver began to bid adieu to its horsecars. Horses were too slow and problematic compared to the speedy and generally dependable cable and electric options. Though horsecars would continue serving through the rest of the century in outlying areas, the city's core would be retrofitted to use the modern methods. The *Denver Times* carried a farewell in 1889, touching as well as illustrative of the great leaps that had been achieved.

> *Looking at the city today it seems barely credible that building a two-mile horsecar line was considered a very bold stroke of business enterprise and an extremely doubtful financial venture* [in the early 1870s], *but the horsecar is now considered an antiquity and the people of Denver are beginning to wonder how they were able to struggle along for so long a time with the slow moving vehicles. They count the days until the city is girded in all directions with cable lines on which they may travel with the speed of the wind. The cry for rapid transit is heard throughout the city and it will be a very short time until horsecars will be banished to the suburbs. Perhaps in the not so distant future the cable cars will share* [their] *fate. Perhaps the electric cars will crowd them out within a similar span of years.*

The reporter's words would prove portentous. In December of that same year, the first electric streetcars appeared in the area, operating on South Broadway.

Before leaving horsecars behind entirely, we relate one of the most endearing aspects of the horsecar era: the Cherrelyn Horsecar. When the

Taken about 1930 at the intersection of Cornell and Broadway, in Englewood, perhaps Deputy Police Chief Les Jordan (holding the front of the streetcar) caught the operator speeding. In actuality, the car is stopped because of a fire (behind the cameraperson), and fire-fighting vehicles are temporarily blocking the streetcar's way. *EPL.*

Denver Tramway discontinued service at the southern end of Broadway, it cut off access to James L. Cherry's "Cherrelyn" subdivision. A gentleman named M.C. Bogue bought the franchise, from Hampden down to Quincy, as well as Horsecar Number 55 from the West Denver Line. After modifying the horsecar's structure, the memorable route began service. The route itself was not the memorable part. That came in the unusual passenger boarding the vehicle for the downhill part of the trek. The first horse to draw the Cherrelyn horsecar was named Quickstep, the route known as the "Cherrelyn Gravity and Bronco Railroad." The horse pulled the horsecar up the hill, stopping and starting, letting passengers on and off as any horsecar would. On the return trip, heading downhill, the horse would be led around to a ramp to board the vehicle itself. The conductor then let gravity do the work, using the brake to make any necessary stop. This was a pretty plush job for the horse at a time when horses were often worked to extremes.

Evidently, the horse in this picture postcard was more interested in something else than in posing for the camera. The famous Cherrelyn offered the horse a ride on the journey back down the hill, letting gravity do the work. Before being refurbished as the Cherrelyn, this vehicle had been horsecar Number 55. *EPL.*

Owing to its tourist appeal, the Cherrelyn remained in service until 1910, far longer than others among the horsecar circuit. When the lease on the land was not renewed, the Cherrelyn was decommissioned and relegated to history. (To see the Cherrelyn today, visit the Englewood Public Library where the Cherrelyn comes complete with a statue of a horse, ready for its ride on Easy Street!)

As more and more lines were being built and new technologies were replacing the old, additional infrastructure was necessary to carry the lines and their passengers. In 1889, the original Sixteenth Street Viaduct, a wooden structure, was completed. The viaduct was to carry the streetcars over the South Platte River and the train yards behind Union Station. In the nine years since Union Depot, as it was then known, had been erected, the expanding rail traffic through the city and region had necessitated more railroad tracks. The area separating the station from the river, to the northwest, was gradually converted to a train yard. Tracks and trains through the area made it dangerous for pedestrians and streetcars alike. The newspapers of the time are filled with accounts of accidents in the area, some of them fatal. At the least, the roughness of driving a horse carriage over the seemingly endless tracks proved to be jarring for everyone aboard. The viaduct allowed the streetcar the simplicity of going over it all. No longer would the streetcars serving the northwestern part of the city be subject to the dangers and high degree of traffic on the ground below them. Denver would eventually build a number of viaducts to lift some of downtown's numbered streets over the train yard.

In 1890, the Denver Tramway installed electric streetcars on Fifteenth Street, and overhead electric line installation continued apace all over the city, despite occasional fears over safety and declarations that the poles and electric lines were unsightly in themselves. Legal challenges had been brought against the company, asserting that though it had had the right to operate electrically powered vehicles using the third-rail system, this did not apply to electricity carried by overhead lines. The case went to court and was settled in the Denver Tramway's favor, but a precedent of legal wrangling over transit had begun. Similar legal gyrations would bedevil the company for many decades to come, for the company would become the source of many complaints even as it provided excellent and comprehensive service.

The Denver Tramway was one of seven companies operating in the city in 1890, with two more soon to add their services to the menu before Denver's citizens. The companies used or had attempted horsecar lines, cable car lines, electric lines, steam dummy (similar in propulsion to a steam-powered train), storage battery systems and electrified third rails. Methods were tried, discarded, improved, updated and more as the transit tempest whirled around the epicenter of Denver's downtown.

In 1891, the numerous companies and transit forms began experiencing more frequent and rancorous conflict. A June meeting led to some agreements on more rational competition. Further, the companies platted out a track system that would lead them into the next century. Some lines would be modified, others abandoned. Certain streets were set aside as scenic byways, where the streetcar would never go. Finding a way to move forward more cohesively was helpful for all involved. This was timely, because demands on the system were increasing. Cities such as Fletcher and Harman, as well as new real estate developments, such as Cook's Addition (the area to the north of City Park), were agitating for connections to Denver. There were still some

The Sixteenth Street Viaduct carried streetcars past Barteldes Seeds and over the Union Station train yards for destinations to the northwest of Denver. The viaduct would leave some lasting marks on downtown Denver, even after the last streetcar used it. Without streetcars to elevate, Denver's viaducts would eventually be torn down as the city sought to beautify its core.

The Granite Building, shown directly behind this streetcar heading southwest on Fifteenth Street, still stands today at the corner of Fifteenth and Larimer. Now known as one of the city's premier shopping areas, within a few years of this photograph being taken, the area would be known as Denver's Skid Row.

disappointments for individual citizens and sections of the metropolitan area, for not every attempt to attract transit met with success, but overall the general trend was one of ever-increasing access and efficiency.

Another bit of history fell into Denver's lap that year. P.T. Barnum had bought property in southwest Denver in 1878, hoping to make the area into an elite residential destination. Lacking available water as well as a connection to Denver, the city of Barnum, named for its founder, didn't become what he had hoped. When he died in 1891, his daughter inherited the property. Mrs. Helen Barnum Buchtel knew it would need transit to prosper. The Denver Lakewood and Golden Railroad ran a branch south from the line that was making its way to Golden, with Mrs. Buchtel contributing $25,000 toward construction. In this way, what would end up being a working-class neighborhood was connected to the rest of the city, allowing for people of all classes and backgrounds to get together. After all, social interactions were as important (if not more) than work for many people.

One of the places where people got together is discussed in Ken Fletcher's *A Mile High and Three Feet Six Wide*. "In 1892 the Tramway opened the Central Loop on 15th Street between Lawrence and Arapahoe. 'Meet me at the Loop' became a phrase that bound south Denver residents to their north Denver friends." The loop offered more than a convenient transfer point where almost all the city's transit came together. It had a celebratory feeling, one that has been commented on by many alive today who recall using it. People shopped, had lunch at the Loop Lunch Room, Gano Senter's Restaurant or the Tramway Cafe and bought groceries and other necessities to take home. It was, for a while, the center of Denver.

The year 1892 also saw passenger service begin on the Denver Lakewood and Golden Railroad, passing through Dry Gulch and the future city of Lakewood (this was one of the interurban railways that would eventually extend Denver's connectivity much beyond its borders). Streetcars also began serving Riverside Cemetery, located north of town, along the South Platte River. They would reach Fairmount Cemetery during the following memorable year. Not only could people ride streetcars to these cemeteries to visit their loved ones who had been lost, but the streetcars could also transport the dead on their final journey. Funeral Car A could be hired to transport the casket and funeral party to the cemetery.

On a more festive note, visitors to the Mile High City could also travel on sightseeing cars, open air during the summer, touring all the most notable spots within Denver. In a city renowned for its sunshine and climate, most people assumed the 1890s would be a banner decade.

Both rail and rubber-tired transit methods are visible at the Central Loop in downtown Denver. This area served for many years as the heart of the city, where people met, shopped, dined and transferred from one line to another.

As the center of Denver's transit function, the Loop offered access to every place served by the Denver Tramway Corporation. Tickets for destinations near and far on the interurban could be acquired at the Interurban Loop Ticket Office.

When the Golden line began regular operation in 1904, a *Denver Post* reporter had this to say: "'Golden! All off!' It was the voice of the cheerful conductor. 'Hoo-ray-y-y!' This was the shout of the people of Golden, who had gathered by the hundred to see the first passenger coach arrive at its destination." The medallion at the front of the vehicle notes that this was a Rocky Mountain Train Club excursion. *RTD.*

The year 1893 would prove to be a watershed year for transit as well as for the whole nation. The General Electric Company perfected a control mechanism for electric streetcars that cemented their ascendency in the fight for technological supremacy. Cable cars remained superior only on particularly long or steep grades. The Denver City Cable Railway, the original provider in Denver, was stuck with cable technology, having heavily invested in it. Conversely, the Denver Tramway had thrown its lot almost entirely into the field of electric vehicles. Though it had a few cable cars still functioning, electric streetcars outnumbered them. Once a promising technology, cable cars were now a superseded and charming relic. The changeover had begun. A greater tumult was brewing on the horizon, however, and this time it was not based on increasing mechanical expertise.

Silver mining, the state's main industry, had made many rich. Many circumstances, international as well as interstate, led to silver's crown losing its luster and historians still debate them. The results of the Crash of 1893, whatever the causes, were widely felt. Half of Denver's banks closed in July of that year. Many formerly wealthy citizens fell from the ranks of the elite to join the hoi polloi, and many who had already been among the bottom echelon were disenfranchised completely. City agencies, like the chamber of commerce, transformed the banks of the South Platte River into a tent city for the unemployed. Innumerable miners, who had gambled on finding gold and silver, were out of luck with half of the state's mines closed.

Streetcar companies suffered as a result. Their success depended on people needing to go somewhere, for work and for pleasure. With so many in the city no longer working, the number of commuters fell. Similarly, travel for pleasure greatly diminished, with every extra nickel being spent on the necessities of life rather than on a streetcar ride to a gathering place one could not afford to enter. Streetcar companies retrenched, cutting staff and cutting service, whatever was necessary to survive. These reductions met with indignation by those thus affected. For example, streetcar service to Montclair ended each night at 6:00 p.m. for a while, meaning that once someone got home, home is where that person would stay! The companies felt some changes had to be made; they were fighting for their lives.

The Denver City Railway Company, deeply in debt, entered receivership in 1896. The courts took over the company. Attempts at retooling the company, even to the point of changing its name twice within two years, ultimately fell short. The failure of the city's first transit company was not without its silver lining: in 1899, the much-renamed Denver Horse Railroad Company merged with its rival, the Denver Consolidated Tramway Company. Where there had once been numerous companies, consolidation dominated the end of the decade. One overarching company rose from the ashes, from the years of competition. The Denver City Tramway Company faced the approaching century alone among all those that had formerly shared the city's landscape. The company moved forward by electrifying all lines and converting all cable cars by 1900.

In just over forty-one years, Denver's transit map had gone from being completely empty to having efficient, reliable and modern electric streetcars connecting every part of the city. The city had endured spasms in technology and joined the ranks of other American cities looking with great expectation to the century ahead. By 1895, electrically powered streetcars totaled more than ten thousand miles of tracks in American cities. So prolific had the construction been in some parts of the nation that one could actually take streetcars from New York to Boston. With one company now at the helm, the citizens of Denver had every reason to believe that a unified vision would lead to great things. In many ways, they were correct. All the same, the seeds of a paradigm-shifting technology were already beginning to sprout across the landscape. These technologies would no longer move on metal rails.

According to author Robert Heilbroner, the first gas-powered automobile appeared in the United States in 1892. Early inventors in this technology, the Duryea Brothers, sold thirteen automobiles in 1896. That same year, an enterprising mechanic, Henry Ford, sold his first "quadricycle," as he then called it. In 1909, he sold over ten thousand automobiles. Just twenty years later, as the Great Depression began to ravage the nation, there were more than twenty-three million cars on American streets, one for every five Americans. Heilbroner continues: "To the average American family [the automobile] became the most prized (and most expensive) of all its possessions, save only its home. It was the means for cheap and easy travel that made Americans, always a restless people, into a nation of motorized vagabonds. It changed the location of industry and of workers' housing, for it was no longer necessary to live within walking distance of work or near a trolley route. It altered urban configurations: the move to the suburbs was made on rubber tires and would have been impossible without them."

As the 1900s dawned, however, this approaching calamity for the streetcar had not yet registered. The Denver City Tramway Company prepared to move full steam—or full electricity, in this case—ahead.

The first decade of the century, which had appeared as if it would be a time of unfettered growth, still came with some weeds in an otherwise beautiful garden. One of the most worrisome and perpetual issues was the company's franchise. Had the franchise been granted in perpetuity, as the Denver City Tramway Company declared, or should it be periodically renegotiated, as the company's detractors insisted? Among the most outspoken of these detractors were the city's primary newspapers. The *Denver Post*, helmed by the Janus-like Frederick Bonfils and Harry Tammen, and the *Rocky Mountain News*, the mouthpiece of Senator Thomas Patterson, lambasted the tramway. The *Denver Post* compared the then-head of the company, William Gray Evans, to Emperor Bonaparte, calling him "Napoleon Bill Evans," and vitriolic sentiments against Evans often appeared daily. Thomas Patterson produced diatribes that were at least somewhat more gentlemanly, contending that monopolies should be publicly owned. Most historians who study Denver's transit past tend to side with the Denver Tramway in this time of strife. Certainly the Denver Tramway was not doing anything that was not standard practice in most American cities. Nevertheless, the first years of the 1900s would not be free of harsh vituperation laid across the streetcars' tracks.

Industrial Denver, a small promotional magazine talking about all the reasons to do business in the Mile High City, naturally chose this view of Seventeenth Street to depict the city's potential. With Union Station at the far end, along with a somewhat fanciful view of the mountains, business owners were sure to be impressed.

While on the subject of William Gray Evans, we note the family's long association with the growth of Denver. Colorado's second territorial governor, John Evans, reached Denver early in its history, in 1862. He was assigned to the post by President Lincoln. He founded the Colorado Seminary in 1864, the institution that would one day become the University of Denver. Later, his son William would tear down his father's home at the corner of Fourteenth Street and Arapahoe to build the offices for the Denver Tramway. The family's strong association with the streetcar would also lend the University of Denver the nickname of "Tramway Tech" in the early 1900s. Many University of Denver students worked as streetcar operators during their college years. However much his family had contributed to the city (William's siblings, Anne and Evan, would shape the city significantly), the first decade of the 1900s would test all his business acumen.

The second volume of *Denver Street Railways* includes an example of the trials Evans and the tramway faced: "Demagoguery, lies and false charges came within a whisker of destroying the company's right to do business [during a vote on the franchise issue held in 1906], despite the fact that the Tramway was widely regarded throughout the transit industry as one of the best-run and best-maintained of such firms in North America, and despite the fact that Denverites knew, or should have known, that their streetcar system gave excellent service."

Though the vote was close, the issue was finally resolved and the company could move forward. If anyone believed the tramway had surmounted all difficulties before it, however, those beliefs were soon to be dashed. Unfortunately, Mother Nature was to add her own invective to the mix during the second decade of the century. One of these came even though *some* in Denver's hierarchy were trying to make a safer, more beautiful city.

One of the greatest figures in Denver's history, Robert Speer, served as mayor from 1904 to 1912 and again from 1916 until his death in 1918. He was a fervent proponent of the "City Beautiful" program, urging Denver's population to work toward civic improvements. Should Denver's citizenry follow the course he would lay out for them, he vowed that Denver would become the Paris of the United States. One of the first things he tackled was the eyesore that was Cherry Creek. Up until that time, the usually tranquil, mostly sand-filled channel of the creek had served a number of unsavory purposes, including dump and toilet. The creek had flooded disastrously a number of times, enough to give it the nickname "the Tiger of the Plains." Speer intended to clean up and tame the beast and began a program to do just that. The creek's channel was straightened and constrained on each side by high, concrete retaining walls. Along the northern edge of the creek's now more manicured course, a fine boulevard graced the city's waterborne gem. Today, the street honors Mayor Speer, bearing his name. Unfortunately, the jewel of Cherry Creek would prove to have some flaws within its precise cuts. The Tiger of the Plains still had teeth and chose a beautiful summer Sunday in 1912 to bare them.

The busiest time for streetcars, especially during the summer, was Sunday, when people were traveling to and from church. Afterward, many people enjoyed the liberty of the weekend in visiting places like Manhattan Beach, on the north shore of Sloan's Lake; Elitch Gardens; and Lakeside, as well as other city parks, growing shadier with each passing year. The afternoon of July 14, 1912, however, brought a deluge to the city. Many city streets, still unpaved, let loose a torrent of mud, sand and gravel that buried streetcar tracks. This was problematic for individual streetcars, but in the very late afternoon, the entire system went down. The heavy downpour caused an outage at the Platte Street powerhouse, leading all streetcars to coast to a halt and sit motionless for more than an hour and a half.

Although the rain had stopped in Denver, it had also fallen upstream in great quantities, all of which raced down the channel of Cherry Creek and into the heart of the city. Bridges over Cherry Creek were temporarily impassable, many severely damaged. Water overtopped Speer's retaining walls in some areas, flooding basements and causing widespread structural harm. Mud and debris covered much of the lower business district, train yards and streetcar tracks. Some, such as the streetcar rails along lower Fifteenth Street, in the South Platte River bottomlands, had as much as ten feet of accumulated detritus. The flood had extensively damaged many bridges. Except for the period during which the power had been cut off, service was continued on most lines without further interruption. As numerous lines crossed the affected bridges, a full return to functionality would take some time.

The creek would rise in inundating rage again in the future, such as after the failure of the Castlewood Canyon Dam in 1933. Eventually, the creation of the Cherry Creek Dam and Reservoir would finally collar the Tiger of the Plains. Since the dam's construction, no devastating flood has occurred on Cherry Creek.

Perhaps intent on showing that her quiver was not yet depleted, Mother Nature let loose another arrow the following year with the Great Blizzard of 1913. The snowfall of early December had initially been at levels the company's plows could handle, the snow being light and dry and of

Turning from Thirteenth Street onto Arapahoe, the streetcar blocks the view of Speer Boulevard and the "Tiger of the Plains," Cherry Creek. The spire of St. Elizabeth's Church, still standing on the Auraria Campus, may be seen in the distance. This is the Cherokee line streetcar, heading to the Loop. Just to the right of the photographer is the headquarters of the tramway.

The Blizzard of 1913 let loose too much snow for the streetcars to handle. By the time it was over, the entire city had been stilled. This streetcar, bound for the Union Depot, would have to await people to dig it out before it would move again. *EPL.*

reasonable amounts. However, on the morning of December 4, the sky came apart. The snow was dense and wet, falling in quantities that could not be countered. As streetcar after streetcar ground to a halt, unable to power through the snow and plagued by grades that were now too icy to overtop, sweeping cars were gradually stilled as well. By the late afternoon of December 5, nothing was moving in the city of Denver.

Fortunately, the powerhouse at Fourteenth Street and Platte was still in operation, providing heat and light for those who chose to remain aboard the streetcars. Many workers were trapped at their places of employment, unable to take the streetcar and finding it unsafe to attempt forging the drifts as individuals.

Once the snow finally stopped, an army of tramway workers and staff descended on the tracks to shovel away the snow. The progress was slow, for the snow was abundant, heavy and complicated by ice accumulated in key rail junctions. Disposing of the snow and feeding the crews were problems almost as daunting. One of the most frustrating problems for the streetcars came from the general public. The streetcar tracks were the first corridors cleared along most roadways, so automobiles, horse-drawn vehicles and pedestrians began using these pathways for their own use. Often with nowhere else to go as streetcars came along behind them, the mash up of pedestrians, streetcars and other vehicles created huge snarls. Ultimately, tramway employees and staff bent their backs to the task of clearing the wider streets as well, in hopes of keeping the general public off the streetcar tracks. The system reached normalcy by the middle of January. The city and its transit provider went on to tackle other issues, though never again would the elements shut the entire system down at once.

We earlier touched on the comportment of the sexes on streetcars. In *Manners and Morals of Victorian America*, we learn how things were changing not only in how the streetcars ran but also in how people interacted while aboard. "Gentlemen formerly rose and offered seats to ladies in streetcars. This practice has fallen into desuetude now for several excellent reasons. One is the increasing independence of women, who compete with men on equal terms in every industrial field, and who, in becoming equals, and competitors, cease to be superiors and, so to speak, royalty. Another is the extreme rudeness of women who accept preferred seats without the slightest inclination of the head, or the very faintest word of thanks." Whether carrying the rude or the considerate, the tramway kept its eye on improving the experience for everyone, partly by increasing speed on certain routes.

Denver Tramway Company workers targeted tracks first to allow passage of the streetcars. The abundance of snow everywhere else, however, led these snow-free areas to be an irresistible temptation for everyone else. The congestion in these small corridors was so intense that the workers had to dig out the roads in their entirety before the streetcars could achieve a modicum of free movement. *EPL.*

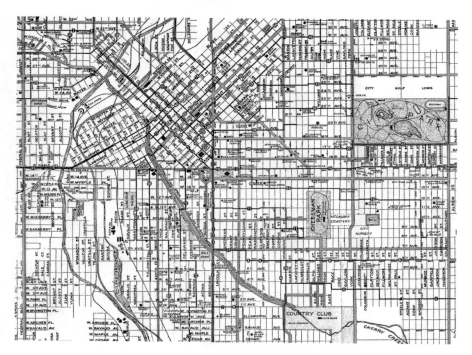

Clason's produced maps for streetcar systems all over the country. This map, from the Clason's Guide for Denver, illustrates just how extensive the system was. At the front of the brochure, Clason's waxed poetic about Denver: "Out where the handclasp's a little stronger, out where the smile dwells a little longer."

INTERURBAN ELECTRIC LINES. Ticket office and station on Arapahoe Street, between Fourteenth and Fifteenth Streets. 37 for list of lines.

INTERURBAN LINES TO SURROUNDING TOWNS

Route No.

82 ARVADA—A town of 915 people, lies in the beautiful Clear Creek Valley, 7 miles from Denver. It is a fertile irrigated farming district. Take Route 81 car at the Interurban Loop.

BOULDER, ELDORADO SPRINGS, LOUISVILLE, MARSHALL and SUPERIOR—Boulder, a city of 10,989 inhabitants, lies in a beautiful irrigated district 30 miles from Denver. The State University of Colorado and the Colorado Chautauqua are located here. Eldorado Springs is a popular summer resort, with swimming pool and many other amusements. Louisville, Marshall and Superior are coal mining towns located in the Northern Coal Field. The Denver & Interurban R. R. cars leave the Union Depot.

83 & 84—GOLDEN—A city of 2484 inhabitants, is located in the foothills, 14 miles west of Denver. Here the State School of Mines has fine buildings located in beautiful grounds. There is an ore testing laboratory and a museum with a fine collection of minerals. The Denver & Inter-Mountain R. R. and Tramway Golden cars leave the Interurban Loop on Arapahoe St. for Golden. Tickets are inter-changeable.

82 LEYDEN—Runs from Interurban Loop past Arvada, to the coal mining town of Leyden. This trip affords a beautiful view of the Rocky Mountains. Fourteen miles.

LITTLETON—Eleven miles from Denver. Take Route 3 car at the Loop. At the end of the line in Englewood, change to the Littleton car.

STREET CAR ROUTES IN NUMERICAL ORDER

Arranged by Streets on Which They Pass Through the Downtown Business District

The forty-odd lines of the Denver Tramway Company all radiate from the downtown district. Transfers are given on all except parallel lines.

THE LOOP—The main tramway loop is on 15th St., between Arapahoe and Lawrence.

ROUTE NUMBERS—Route numbers of each line are posted on the front of cars.

CITY PARK CARS—Take route 40 or 50.

RED ROUTE SIGNS signify cars which serve Union Station. These are indicated by the letter "R" on the list below.
*Goes into Central Loop.

FIFTEENTH STREET LINES

Route No.

*2 Broadway
*3 Englewood
R 4 4th Avenue
*6 6th Avenue
*10 Colfax-Aurora (14)
*10 Colfax-Fairmont (15)
R 29 W. 29th Ave.-So. Gaylord
*66 Stockyards

SIXTEENTH STREET LINES

R 7 Berkeley-So. Pearl
R 8 Berkeley-University Park
R 23 W. 23rd Ave.-25th Ave.
R 28 28th Ave.-W. 44th Ave.
R*37 Rocky Mountain Lake
R*38 W. 38th Avenue
R 39 Argo-19th Ave.

SEVENTEENTH STREET LINES

Route No.

R 11 11th Avenue
R 13 13th Avenue
R 40 Park Hill

EIGHTEENTH STREET LINES

50 22nd Ave.-Kalamath
R 58 Louisiana

CROSS-TOWN AND UNCLASSIFIED LINES

61 Larimer
64 E. 34th Avenue
64 Lawrence
72 Cherokee
*73 Burlington Shops
*74 Globeville
*75 Barnum

35

The Clason's Guide listed the full menu of routes serving Denver and surrounding communities. The numbers would change over time for some.

The cover of the Clason's Guide, showing a view along Sixteenth Street in Denver, would have had different images for each city it served. Any city that had a streetcar would have had a Clason's Guide. Visitors would have recognized the color and format, buying the guide to help them navigate unfamiliar territory.

The year 1913 saw the tramway attempting to speed things up in some ways, even though the year might be best remembered overall for the dramatic slowdown caused by the blizzard. It experimented with "express" streetcars to speed up the transit time between downtown and points on East Colfax. Streetcars heading east stopped at every intersection, even during rush-hour commutes, which resulted in much slower service to the city of Aurora (the former city of Fletcher) and the Montclair neighborhood. An attempted "skip-stop" method of pausing only at every other street in certain parts of town, which would have sped up the commute, was halted by city council. Citizens were outraged at having to walk an extra block. Except for a brief implementation during the First World War, at the behest of the federal government, this sensible method of speeding up transit, so prosaic today for bus travelers, would not be put into place until the 1940s. As Henry Ward Beecher so famously said, "The philosophy of one century is the common sense of the next." The folks at the tramway were clearly visionaries, willing to innovate and experiment in their unremitting efforts to improve service. One of the main ways to improve service, in everyone's opinion, was to speed the commute. The story of the streetcar now begins to speed up significantly, though in a direction few at the Denver City Tramway Company would have guessed during the thriving days of the 1910s. This increasing velocity, this ever-quickening pace of life, had many fans, as represented by one of the greatest visionaries of the twentieth century.

Personally created by Walt Disney himself for the 1964–65 World's Fair in New York, the Carousel of Progress may be enjoyed by those visiting the Tomorrowland section at Disney World. Following a typical American family through decades of technological progress, the views of labor as the 1800s gave way to the 1900s seem quaint to us today. One of the marvels that the mother in the show most admires is the washing machine. "Now I can complete the washing in just two days instead of a week!" she revels. Few in the United States today who have not done a stint in Peace Corps or similar service group comprehend the sense of awe and delight that would have greeted the timesaving devices of a century ago. Among the most breathtaking of these was the automobile. Denver's streetcar company, continually improving its own function, would ultimately provide this adversary, the private automobile, with a tool that would contribute to the streetcar's undoing: ease of access.

In 1914, the company changed its name to the one that would become synonymous with Denver's streetcar history: simply, the Denver Tramway Company. Also that year, the tramway began replacing the Larimer-Colfax

Viaduct, which had previously been restricted to streetcar use. By 1914, the old structure had been deemed insufficient for reasons of safety and, most importantly, access issues. It could not be used by pedestrians, horse-drawn vehicles or automobiles. Non-streetcar users were forced to travel through the Bottomlands, as the area along the South Platte River was known, "an unattractive neighborhood [with] dangerous railroad crossings that had claimed a number of lives."

The opening of the viaduct to all forms of traffic, that ease of access, helped in the short term but was deleterious over the long. Automobile traffic was increasing steadily, and the new viaduct greatly enhanced accessibility in and out of Denver. As *Denver's Street Railways* explains it, "Streetcars were far less costly and [a] much safer means of transport than the private automobile. However, more and more people seemed to be willing to accept the much higher cost of operating their own automobile, along with the reduced safety factor for the sake of the greater door-to-door convenience, easier personal scheduling, and the feeling of pride implicit in automobile ownership. The Denver City Tramway Company provided one of the finest street-railway services anywhere in North America; however, the company found that this service would be hard put to compete with the love affair that was fast developing between Americans and their automobiles."

The streetcar, formerly the bastion of everything modern, began to lose its vaunted place in public opinion. As one contemporary wrote, "Street cars are equipped with all the modern conveniences, including hot and cold conductors and running transfers; this modern octopus rules the great highways of our teeming cities with an iron hand and a steal franchise." The Tramway Company's general manager, John Beeler, had detected the first whiffs of a change in the wind. Between the spring of 1914 and the early autumn of 1915, automobile traffic into and out of downtown Denver had increased 50 percent, while streetcar patronage had shrunk by 9 percent. Though not the tolling bell of death for the streetcar, Beeler and others who were paying attention knew that a shift in transportation modes was forthcoming.

In order to offset the loss in income, the tramway attempted to increase the rate charged for a ride, which was still five cents, as it had been in 1885. The increase in fare was bitterly fought at numerous levels, and these scuffles would continue until 1927. Nor were these debates to be the worst of it. The years before the fare issue was settled in 1927 would hold some terrible times for the company and city, as the previously relatively harmonious relations between management and company labor blew up over wages, working

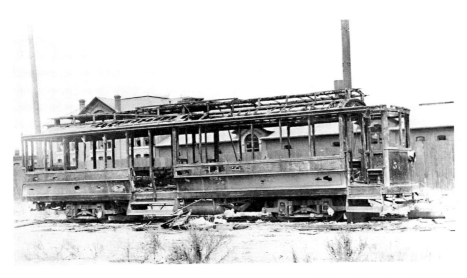

The aftermath of the 1920 strike was more than just seven dead. A number of cars had been vandalized, and some had even been burned. The Union Pacific Shops are in the background, at Fortieth and Franklin. *CRM.*

Operators of streetcars during the strike were told to offer no resistance to mobs. They should get their passengers to safety and leave the streetcars to their fate. *CRM.*

hours, working conditions and whether to unionize. The strike of 1919 was a blissfully peaceful episode in comparison to the strike of August 1920, which saw seven people killed in gun violence between strikebreakers and the angry citizens of Denver. Violence was not restricted to doing harm to people; a number of streetcars were vandalized, and some were even burned. The offices of the *Denver Post*, which had sided with the Denver Tramway Company, were ransacked. Though the strike ended, the costs had been extreme. The financial burdens on the company, coupled with the costs of upkeep and repair, set the company back so severely that it looked around for any innovative solution it could find.

Above: To the left of the operator is a sign reminding transit riders just how good they have it. "In 346 major U.S. cities transit fare is 10¢ or higher; Chicago 17¢; Pittsburgh 15¢; Kansas City 13¢; Des Moines, Detroit, Baltimore, Cincinnati and Tacoma, all 12¢. At today's high costs the 10¢ fare is a bargain." *RTD*.

Opposite, top left: Old habits and laws for navigating Denver streets were no longer adequate when the number of automobiles began to rise. *The Official Denver Municipal Traffic Code*, published in 1940, sought to educate an increasingly self-propelled public.

Opposite, top right: With streetcars still a very common sight on Denver streets, automobile drivers needed to know how their vehicles fit in with the fixed-rail monarchs of the past.

Opposite, bottom: Regardless of the many decades, the logo of the Denver Tramway Corporation is still visible on the side of this old trolley coach.

A Message to Denver Motorists and Pedestrians

The traffic rules contained herein have been drafted for the protection of YOU Mr. Motorists and of YOU Mr. Pedestrian. The Police Department is endeavoring to enforce these rules fairly, impartially and to the letter, solely for the purpose of protecting the lives and property of our citizens.

The ever-increasing number of automobiles presents a traffic problem which must be shared by all alike. 100,000 automobiles operate on Denver's streets. At least one-half of our population look upon the car as a necessity, therefore, traffic laws should be studied and understood by both the motorist and pedestrian for their own welfare and protection. We must make sure that our traffic engineering and educational work in safety obtains results. Effective enforcement of traffic regulations is necessary to secure the benefits of this program. The greater majority of drivers and pedestrians will obey reasonable laws and regulations, the remainder must be compelled to do so for the safety of the public as a whole.

Mr. and Mrs. Motorist and Mr. and Mrs. Pedestrian upon reading these traffic ordinances, we trust that you will be convinced that they have been promulgated FOR YOUR SAFETY and are not devised to impose a hardship on anyone. The Police who have been charged with enforcing the traffic code, appeal to every person using our streets to develop good driving and walking habits and to voluntarily observe the regulations contained herein, thereby doing your part toward making Denver the SAFEST CITY.

Assuring you that the Police Department's only interest is that pertaining to your convenience, comfort and safety, we earnestly request your full cooperation in the observance of these regulations.

Respectfully yours,
WM. E. GUTHNER,
Manager of Safety & Excise.

SECTION 18
Pedestrians Soliciting Rides

It shall be unlawful for any person to stand in a roadway for the purpose of soliciting a ride from the operator of any private vehicle.

ARTICLE V—Street Cars and Railroad Trains
SECTION 19
Passing Street Cars

(a) The operator of a vehicle shall not overtake and pass upon the left any street car proceeding in the same direction, whether actually in motion or temporarily at rest. This provision shall not apply on one-way street nor to the passing of a street car on a single track line, which track is to the right of the center of the street.

(b) The operator of a vehicle overtaking any street car stopped or about to stop for the purpose of receiving or discharging any passenger shall stop such vehicle to the rear of the nearest running board or door of such street car and keep it stationary until any such passenger has boarded such street car or reached a place of safety, except that where a safety zone has been established, a vehicle need not be stopped before passing any such street car but may proceed past such street car at a speed not greater than is reasonable and safe, not exceeding the rate of ten (10) miles per hour, and with due caution for the safety of pedestrians. This provision shall not apply to passing upon the left of any street car on a one-way street.

SECTION 20
Driving on Street Car Tracks

(a) It shall be unlawful for the operator of any vehicle proceeding upon any street car tracks in front of a street car upon a public street to fail to remove such vehicle from the tracks as soon as practicable after signal from the operator of such street car.

(b) When a street car has started to cross an intersection, no operator shall drive upon or across the car tracks within the intersection in front of the street car.

SECTION 21
Driving Through Safety Zone Prohibited

It shall be unlawful for the operator of a vehicle at any time to drive the same over or through any part of a safety zone as defined in this ordinance.

14

One of the solutions settled on was the use of trolley coaches (powered as the streetcars were) and buses. Buses had been in operation on East Colfax, from the end of the Colfax Line to Fitzsimons Army Hospital, since 1919. The tramway attempted to introduce buses into its cadre of service vehicles in 1925, but voters declined the change. The tramway was unrelenting, however. Under the auspices of a weakened viaduct at Twenty-third Street, the company transformed its Globeville services from streetcar to bus. The Denver Tramway Corporation, as it became known in 1925, began buying bus transit companies as streetcars continued to vanish in non-core regions of the metropolitan area. By 1940, the trend was incontrovertibly obvious; this was the year when Sixteenth Street, the heart of Denver's shopping district, converted from streetcar to trolley coach (with a bus here and there). Those in Denver would have needed only to look to the nation as a whole to find confirmation. In *Light Rail and Heavy Politics*, we learn, "In Colorado, as in most of the country, trolleys vanished first in smaller towns and cities. Boulder, Cripple Creek, Colorado Springs, Grand Junction and Greeley had all lost their lines by the late 1930s. Fort Collins' municipally owned system proved an exception to this general trend, hanging on until 1951."

The first trolley coaches were powered by using the same overhead electric lines that powered the streetcars. These too would gradually find themselves shuffled into retirement; in 1948, diesel-powered buses were introduced. The system had 131 streetcars in service, 138 electrically powered buses and 116 buses using diesel fuel. *Denver's Street Railways* indicates that "[as] early as 1948, the Denver Tramway Corporation had announced detailed plans to convert all its streetcar routes to trolley coach and bus operation. A large crowd of protesters attended a hearing in January of 1950 [to speak out against the removal of the streetcar]." The technological rush forward would not be stopped, however, by those isolated voices who wished to keep the streetcar. The *Denver Post*, in 1947, referred to the streetcars as congested trams that plagued Denver citizens. In 1948, the *Denver Post* asked if the streetcars offered "sardines or service?"

Darrell Arndt, who we will revisit in Chapter Three, illustrated some of the feelings guiding people's decisions at that time.

You have to understand that in the 1950s, it was exciting to look at new car models. You anticipated the arrival of new models, talked about changes, as if the cars were Hollywood stars. The car dealerships capitalized on this love affair. Showrooms would have paper on the windows to prevent people seeing inside, then there would be the dramatic unveiling. My family moved

For the past several years officials of the City and County of Denver and the Denver Tramway Corporation have worked closely together to bring about a modernization of the city's transit system.

Saturday, June 3, 1950—the date of this publication—marks the retirement of all street cars and the complete conversion of the system to rubber-tired vehicles. Completion of this program is the most significant step taken in the development of Denver's transportation system since the horse car appeared on its streets in 1871.

Less than two years ago it was thought that the program now completed could not possibly be finished before 1953. It is, therefore, a real pleasure for me now to congratulate the Denver Tramway Corporation upon its remarkable achievement in reaching the desired goal so far ahead of schedule and to congratulate Mr. Earl Mosley, former Director of Utilities for the City of Denver, for his constructive role in this accomplishment.

Denver now has one of the finest surface transit systems .in the country.

QUIGG NEWTON

Mayor of Denver

Left: For Mayor Newton, the removal of the streetcars was not something to lament. It was seen as a bold step forward, especially since its conclusion came in ahead of schedule. Despite Mayor Newton's optimism, the times ahead would still offer significant challenges for Denver.

Below: The trolley coaches serving the metropolitan region were powered like the streetcars, via a connection to the overhead wire. In this image, taken about 1950, the flexible arm is easily visible rising from the top of the vehicle. *EPL.*

to the suburbs of Chicago in 1950, so we had to have a car, but as a young man, I was also excited about cars.

On June 3, 1950, the final streetcars made their journeys across Denver's rails. The "automobile was not the only villain as far as declining patronage was concerned," *Denver's Street Railways* reminds us. New technologies, such as radio, allowed people to enjoy more activities at home, when they used to go out for such festivities. People used their cars to reach plays, movies, amusement parks and one another. *Denver's Street Railways* continues: "Patience was growing thin with the Tramway's ancient streetcars. Compared with the sleek, new [buses], replete with comfortable seats, rapid acceleration and curbside service, the old wooden cars, some dating back to 1903, seemed to be almost an embarrassment for some residents of the city." Everything in life needed to be modern during the boom times following the Second World War; streetcars did not fit into the future as most Americans envisioned it. Modernization costs money, however, and with fewer people taking public transit, the funds available were growing as thin as the patience of Denver's citizens. Ceremonies were held on June 3, dignitaries spoke and many people boarded streetcars for one final go. Emblazoned across the front of the streetcars, with a humanized streetcar letting loose a tear, the words "Good-bye, old friends" heralded the change ahead.

Despite this tearful farewell on behalf of Denver's streetcars, in his book *Transportation for Cities: The Role of Federal Policy*, Wilfred Owens would have watched them depart with dry eyes indeed:

> *The reason for preferring private over public transit is not, as often alleged, the perversity of the consumer or his ignorance of economics. Part of the reason can be ascribed to public policy that has favored the car, but the basic reason why most urban trips are made by automobile is that the family car, despite its shortcomings, is superior to any other method of transportation. It offers comfort, privacy, limited walking, minimum waiting, and freedom from schedules or routing. It guarantees a seat; protects the traveler from heat, cold, and rain; provides space for baggage; carries extra passengers at no extra cost; and for most trips, except those in the center city, gets there faster and cheaper than any other way. The transit rider confronts an entirely different situation. He must walk, wait, stand, and be exposed to the elements. The ride is apt to be costly, slow, and uncomfortable because of antiquated equipment, poor ventilation, and service that is congested in rush hours, infrequent during any other time of day, inoperative at night, and non-existent in suburbs.*

Even as their demise was being helped along by automobiles, streetcars had to play host to advertisements extolling the latest improvements to their rivals. The 1950 Ford came with "automatic overdrive," something you surely did *not* get to enjoy while riding a streetcar. *RTD.*

Coming northeast on Larimer, between Fifteenth and Sixteenth Streets, the streetcar carries the placard indicating its final run: Good-bye old friends. Like the streetcar, the buildings in this picture had a short time to remain. None of the buildings in this picture would survive Denver's efforts at urban renewal during the 1950s and 1960s. The stone building at the end of the block contained some of the offices of the railroad.

As streetcars were being replaced, the Denver Tramway Corporation sought to put a positive spin on the change. A new bus would be replacing this old vehicle, with all of the associations that the word "new" carried with it. *CRM.*

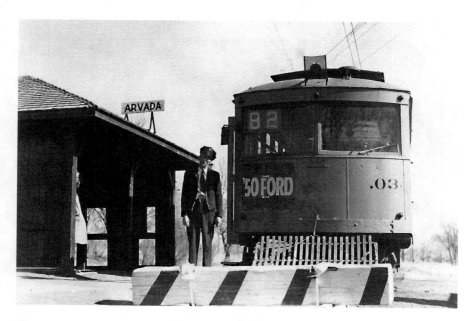

The shelter to the left of the interurban would have kept a person out of the rain but not temperature extremes. This exposure to the elements was cited as one of the primary detractions of streetcars. People in their automobiles, it was assumed, suffered no such privations. *RTD.*

Looking east out of Civic Center Park, toward the capitol, a streetcar occupies what was then a two-way street, Broadway. The streetcar is decked out with bunting to call attention to it on the final day streetcars would be running. *RTD.*

Owens's point of view is shared by many, but not all.

Historian Kenton Forrest, whom we will meet in Chapter Two, and his colleagues, in the book *Mile-High Trolleys*, offered a summation of this transition, as well as a thought on the future that yet lay ahead:

> *The Denver Tramway Corporation found itself in a position common to most transit systems in mid century. The pressure of rising costs against diminishing revenues as riders took to their automobiles required even higher fares and continuing reductions in service, a chain reaction which the most ingenious management cannot reverse. With millions spent to improve a highway system that never quite catches up to demand, it now seems time to reexamine our outlook upon the task of transporting the population to and from work each day and to reconsider the responsibility of government to aid private enterprise in this endeavor. Perhaps we shall again witness steel wheels moving swiftly along a network of rails serving our city. If ever this occurs, it will be ample proof that the big yellow cars were really not so antiquated.*

When the streetcar ended its run in 1950, a plaque was put up in Civic Center Park. Located just to the southeast of the Voorhies Memorial, it reads, "The plaque commemorates the passing of the streetcar, which served the city's transit needs for nearly eighty years, starting with the horse car, December 17, 1871. The plaque is placed here near the site of the large cable house, which provided power for transit lines during the era when the Welton Street Line was one of the longest street car cable lines in the world: 65,600 feet."

Published in 1975, these prophetic words will lead us to the face of transit in Denver in the modern day. Before we leave the streetcar behind entirely, however, we now give voice not to the historians who have made transit their fondest study but to those average citizens who knew the streetcar as a part of their daily lives.

CHAPTER 2

WHERE WE CONNECTED
WITH EACH OTHER

It is undeniable that isolation was often a pervasive part of life in the frontier West. Great distances and the harshness of winters without modern comforts and tools exacerbated an already common quandary. Nevertheless, there were many ways in which the "good old days" were more interactive than they are today. In the days prior to ubiquitous computers, televisions, cell phones, movie theaters and the like, people had more of a reason to be together as work and life permitted it. In the book *The Mirror*, by Marlys Millhiser, a young woman living in Boulder, Colorado, in 1978 is transported against her will back to the year 1900. Pulling into the nearby town of Nederland on a horse-drawn wagon, she notices people on the front porches of the houses along their route. Asking her companion why everyone is sitting outside, he replies, "It's a nice evening. What else should they be doing?" She doesn't respond aloud, privately concluding that everyone should be inside watching television. The arrival of more and more electronic modes of entertainment in the 1900s allowed for more time to be spent in the company of other people without actually interacting with them.

The spread of public transportation throughout cities in the United States in the 1800s and first half of the 1900s countered this drift toward separation. Transit facilitated much more than *getting* someplace; it allowed for people to get out and get together. In the words of one of the people interviewed for this book, it was "where we connected with each other."

If radios, television and movies had been among the only significant forces allowing people less interactions in cities, the unifying effect of the streetcars might well have lasted to the modern day. These technological marvels were *not* alone, however; they were overshadowed by that greatest nail in the streetcars' coffin: automobiles. As we will discuss in Chapter Three, the influence of the automobile directly determined the decline in use of public transportation in the United States, and its importance cannot be exaggerated.

Still, the removal of the streetcars in the Denver region was not undertaken without having some form of public transit there to replace them. Buses filled the gap and, for many people, continue to be a primary method of getting around today. Initially seen as modern and without the limitations of streetcars restricted to metal tracks, buses nevertheless lacked something in many people's estimations. An entire sensory experience was gone. At the time of this writing, it is more than sixty-two years since the last passengers were conveyed about Denver by the streetcar. Thus, the people who actually *remember* riding the streetcar are being lost to us through gradual attrition. This chapter will put down in writing some of the impressions and memories of those people before they are lost to us forever. In addition, one of those who has made transit his life's passion will be featured, not as the content specialist he is normally considered to be, but as transit taker himself. All these voices have helped to perpetuate the streetcar's history for future generations, even after the *clackity-clack* of the streetcar was silenced at the end of the line.

Please note that the filter of numerous years sometimes dilutes the accuracy of one's memory; the personal recollections here shared have not been altered in the case of minor discrepancies.

For Charles A., riding the streetcar was one of the most exciting things to do, sometimes even more than the actual destination itself. Born in 1942, Charles would have been eight when the streetcars concluded their service.

My family lived about half a block west of York. On the other side of York was City Park. Whenever my family and I needed to go downtown, we always rode the streetcar. I especially liked sitting in the back. Though the majority of the seats were separated by an aisle running down the middle of the car, in the back there was a curved seat that hugged the entire rear of the streetcar. When the streetcar went around a corner, the back of the vehicle would swing out, and the force would make us slide along the seat. Of course, as kids, we encouraged the sliding a little bit, and that was great fun. It was very exciting. In the summertime you could smell the brakes. The occasional sparks from the wheels on the track made a scent like ozone, which I remember very well. The whole journey was an event.

Living so close to the tracks of the streetcar, Charles could hear its not-so-distant passage during summer nights when his windows would be open. He could imagine all the people going places, for the streetcars always seemed to be quite full, especially to a child.

When World War II ended, everyone gathered downtown to celebrate. I remember being stunned that there were so many people. I could not imagine how there could be so many people, and many of them were getting downtown on the streetcars. The streetcars were full of celebration and good feeling as well. I was very young, but I remember the enormity of the experience. That was a time when the streetcar was something very special, but most of the time it was just a commonplace part of your day. Everyone took the streetcar, so you didn't think about it being something special, something that you would lose. All levels of society were there, all types of people were on the streetcar. You would go to work, to school, to a movie and that was just regular life. My mother would take us to the Loop Market quite a bit because it was so convenient; she shopped there all the time.

Though the buses that replaced the trolleys were fascinating for Charles in their way, he remembers feeling sorry to see the streetcars go away.

I live in Washington Park now, so I don't use the Light Rail much, but when I do I always enjoy it. I feel that we're going through a renaissance for transit in the United States. Having this system is a great benefit for Denver, and I still find joy in taking the train. Every time I go, it is an adventure!

Though they did not know each other, Colleen P. grew up quite close to Charles. Her home was at Sixteenth Avenue and Garfield Street, just south of City Park. She was fourteen when the streetcars were removed from Denver's cityscape.

I never could understand why we needed to "modernize," but I guess that was life then. It is the same way now, of course. The streetcars were replaced by electric buses. They were pretty much the same except that they were quieter. Still, it was great fun to ride the streetcar. It was kind of bumpy and noisy. Everyone went downtown to shop in the lovely stores, go to the movies and restaurants; most of the exciting things to do were downtown, though we would sometimes go to the University of Denver campus stadium to see the football games. Some of the Denver high schools played their games there. We rode the streetcar wherever we were going. In addition to reaching our actual destination, we discovered things along the way, so the journey itself was special. On our way to the University of Denver I discovered the Bonnie Brae Tavern, with its topnotch pizza.

Colleen describes how the streetcar was more than just a conveyance; it was a sort of amusement for those with a creative mindset. Kids were always hanging out the windows to see if they could get the streetcar to rock. Boys would put spare cents on the tracks.

When the trolley car came by, it would flatten them—the coins, not the boys—and that was good fun. I don't know much about the history of the streetcar, but I have a lot of nostalgia for it.

Born in 1932, Fred H. grew up in Denver, remaining here until he went to college in Boulder. As with many children, he rode the trolley car alone at a very early age.

In the early '40s I was riding the streetcar by myself. Everyone used the streetcar, but in World War II, with all the rationing of gas and rubber, people used them even more. We had a car, but we did not use it much. Streetcars and buses were our main transportation. We lived in the eastern part of Denver at Twelfth Avenue and Syracuse, in some homes for non-commissioned officers. We would walk over to Colfax and Poplar for the Number 14 streetcar because that is where it turned around to go back downtown. If you were heading east of there, you would take a bus. We rode downtown to the Loop. I remember riding along Sixteenth Street, long before there was a mall there. Everyone used the streetcar and used it for everything.

Being a child, Fred paid a different fare from what the adults paid, sometimes using coins and sometimes using the small tokens that the transit company produced. In his memory, the streetcars were large and yellow, easily seen at any distance, and indicative of a journey about to begin.

I went to Smiley Junior High School. I was a sweeper boy in the school, helping the janitor. When I was just going to school I would take the school bus, but on the days when I worked, I took the streetcar. I worked there until I finished ninth grade, which was still at Smiley then, and after I transferred to East for high school. Sometimes I caught a ride, but most of

Taken from the D&F Clock Tower, looking southeast along Sixteenth Street, the automobiles sharing the roadway with the streetcars illustrate what Denver's main commercial strip would have looked like before it was made into a pedestrian mall served by a shuttle. The domed building farther in the distance is the capitol. The other domed structure, closer to the viewer and to the right, was the Arapahoe County Courthouse. Though the courthouse is gone, its memory is still honored in a street name: Court Place. *DMF.*

the time I used the streetcar. The streetcar was not only for work, though. On Saturday mornings I would take the streetcar to go to the Aladdin Theater, or maybe the Ogden or Bluebird. The Bluebird was a neighborhood theater then. At ten in the morning there would be a short subject, some kind of serial that you could watch, with characters like cowboys. Then there would be two cartoons and a double feature. Once we got there, we stayed all day, not getting home until it was time for dinner.

Fred remembers how the streetcars were vulnerable to mischief, especially as they were going around corners. At that point, the line connecting the top of the trolley to its power source, the wire above, would be stretched to its greatest length, which meant that pulling it down was also at its easiest.

If a kid timed it just at the right moment, he could run over from the curb and pull the wires down, disconnecting them from above. Of course, at that point, the trolley could not move any more. I was with a group once that did that, though I just watched. The conductor had to get someone to come and help him, because he didn't have the equipment to do it himself, and that took maybe fifteen or twenty minutes. He was really angry, but we were watching from far enough away to be able to run. That was a popular recreation for the kids, though now that I think of it, it was probably not so much fun for the folks trying to get somewhere.

Fred and his family also did things together that involved the streetcar. The function of transit in those days was not only to get folks to work but also to get them to the enjoyable offerings around town. Fred and his family would ride the streetcar to Elitch Gardens as well as Lakeside Amusement Park, with a switch downtown for the line heading to the northwestern part of the city. Downtown also offered shopping and the occasional trip to the capitol to head up to the dome for the view.

The streetcars were not that comfortable. They had rattan seats and were rough because the metal wheels didn't offer any cushion. The seats were straight and rigid, with no cushions on them. It was not comfortable, but I was a kid and was not concentrating on comfort. The streetcars were not elegant, but they offered everyone a way to go somewhere for an affordable price. There were distractions on the streetcar, too; they published a little booklet called As-You-Go, *which would have jokes and other things like that. I liked to read that.*

Depending on the time of day, the streetcars could be quite full. There were students going to and from school as well as adults going to and from work.

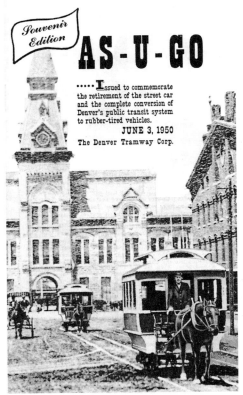

Above: Route 61, which traveled through downtown Denver on Larimer, proudly announces Nickel Day at Elitch's. Amusement parks were one of the most popular reasons for using the streetcars, providing door-to-park service. *RTD.*

Left: Published from the 1930s until the time of the streetcars' departure, *As-You-Go* would entertain readers with bits of news, jokes and items of useful information. This commemorative edition was put out to celebrate just how far the city had come. Note the horsecar shown on the front cover.

The buses that replaced the streetcars were not necessarily more comfortable than what had come before, but I wasn't really around for the transition. When the streetcars were being removed, I was leaving to begin my studies in Boulder. So I was not necessarily sad to see them go; I thought that whatever was easiest was fine.

As an adult, Fred would have another association with transit, though the streetcars of his youth were by that time long gone. Working for Channel 7 News in Denver in the early 1980s, he was primarily assigned to cover the goings-on of the statehouse. Ancillary to that was the "transportation beat," and he did a documentary covering the prospect of adding an electric train to Denver. Later, with Channel 2, he traveled to cities in the United States like San Francisco and Atlanta and even visited Edmonton, Alberta.

You'd expect people to be divided on whether or not we should have a train put back in Denver, but I was surprised by how strong the emotions were, both pro and con. No one was diffident about sharing an opinion! I interviewed people around the U.S. and Canada. My own opinion was that this was something we should really have. In the late 1970s, when I went to a news conference in Washington, D.C., I even got to ask President Carter why some cities in the United States had transit, but we did not here in Denver. He had a good political answer, but it was not really an answer at all. When the train finally got going in Denver, people were arguing even then. Some complained it was not coming to their neighborhoods, and others complained that it was, because that would destroy their neighborhoods, they felt. This kind of arguing has been going on forever, but all the same, I am glad we have it. One day I will no longer be able to drive. I will be glad to have the trains when I want to go to a game or something else downtown.

In a city full of streets, most may never be driven on even by lifelong residents of the city, but there are a few that everyone is sure to drive at least sometimes, if not often. One of these would definitely be Colfax Avenue. Designated Highway 40 by the federal government, Colfax was dubbed "the longest, wickedest street in the United States" by Playboy Magazine. Though it no longer reaches from Atlantic City, New Jersey, to Oakland, California, it's still a street with a lot of history. In Denver and in some of the towns in the eastern part of the state, nineteenth-century politician Schuyler Colfax would still find his eponymous street were he to visit today. For most people in Denver in the 1800s and first half of the 1900s, however, Colfax was an everyday street, residential in character for much of its length. The transition into car-serving proto-highway, begun in the 1920s, would reach its zenith in the middle of the century. Until the interstate system sent Colfax Avenue into a many-decade plummet out of the city's esteem, it was the primary artery for folks heading west or east through the metropolitan area.

Jean D. moved into the Mayfair neighborhood of Denver in 1942, when she was five years old. Since her family did not own a car, the streetcar along Colfax was the only mode of transportation into and out of downtown.

I remember Colfax as being a narrow street, with both Fourteenth and Thirteenth Avenues being two-way streets. Thirteenth Avenue wasn't even paved. We took the Number 14 trolley on Colfax for everything. My father rode it to his work at Fifteenth Street and Tremont. There was a while when he had two jobs, leaving early in the morning and catching the last trolley at night. He often fell asleep along the way, so would miss his stop, ending up at the end of the route. Then he would have to ride back, trying to stay awake so that he didn't end up downtown once more. My mother would load me on the trolley for shopping day downtown at the Denver Dry, Daniels and Fishers, Neusteters and Woolworths. There were no shopping centers and downtown Denver was "the place" to shop. My special reward was when my mother would take me to Woolworths, after shopping, for lunch and a sweet treat. We would load the trolley with our purchases to our stop on Jasmine Street.

The family's other major use of the trolley was to get to church on Fourteenth and Birch. While they walked there most of the time, Jean enjoyed the luxury of getting to ride the trolley sometimes. The decision to ride was based on whether the family had enough money for the fare.

We had friends that lived in North Denver. My mother always brought food, so we would load the trolley, being careful not to spill or destroy the bags of food she would take. We had to transfer downtown to another trolley as the Number 14 only serviced the East Colfax corridor. We would have to check the schedule, at the transfer site, to determine which trolley to take and where to stand to board. There was an additional fare for each time you would board a trolley unless you had a transfer, which allowed you to go from one trolley line to another. It seemed as if we were going on an adventure each time we went to North Denver. I believe it took us an hour or more to get to our destination. We had to watch our time to leave North

Perhaps a proud father posing with his sons during off-duty hours, the line to and from Golden carried workers into downtown Denver for work and play. With hats like those a streetcar operator might wear, the boys might have imagined themselves at the helm of such a vehicle one day. *RTD.*

Denver to catch the last trolley to downtown. Sometimes one friend, who had a car, would take us to the transfer station. Most of the time, we had to take the trolley all the way home.

Jean's family would usually buy tokens to use for their trips, though regular coins could be used as well. Though Jean's recollections of her years on the streetcar are more factual than some, they nevertheless demonstrate the seamless integration of transit into daily life for many Denverites. Some memories concerning the streetcars demonstrate just the opposite: the sensory experience of the ride.

This image taken by the Public Health Building, just off Sixth Avenue, shows the area near Denver General Hospital. Patients could take the streetcar to get to the hospital and pick up something at the pharmacy afterward to help them feel better! *Denver Health.*

For Jean H., who lived at Forty-fourth Avenue and Decatur Street in 1946, when she was a five-year-old girl, the streetcar numbers and routes are lost and meaningless minutiae in the face of powerful reminiscences.

> *I remember that streetcar garage* [the Loop] *at about Fourteenth Street and Lawrence and the thrill of eating there. They had round tables. My most vivid memory is from when my mother had to take me to Children's Hospital on the streetcar. I was going to have my tonsils removed. I was excited to be riding the streetcar, though that did not overshadow the anxiety of having to be alone at the hospital.*

For Joyce T., who grew up by Twenty-second Avenue and Grape Street, the end of the line was nearby, at Hudson Street and Twenty-third Avenue, so she thought the streetcar was very convenient. She didn't have to worry about falling asleep on the line. If she missed her stop, she was only two blocks from home when the streetcar paused at its terminus.

> *The only bad part about falling asleep on the streetcar was the woven seats. I would fall asleep leaning against them and have the pattern temporarily imbedded in my face, so when I got home, everyone knew I had been dozing. I took the streetcar from an early age. It was free until you were five, but we cheated for a long time. I did not start paying until I was wearing lipstick.*

Even as a young child, Joyce would go all over the place completely alone, even downtown Denver. She felt very safe. Her father would take her to the Republic Building for dental appointments. Once safely ensconced with the dentist, her father would leave to do his own errands.

1660. Sixteenth Street from Arapahoe Street, Denver, Colo.

This picture postcard shows the view along Sixteenth Street to the southeast, with the state capitol in the distance. Though some of the buildings shown in this view are still along the 16th Street Mall today, the Tabor Grand Opera House, with its dramatically peaked black roof, is sadly not one of them.

The dentist would give me a nickel if I was good. I would then wander around downtown, entertaining myself, until I found Temple Emmanuel. Once I was there, I knew where I was and would hop on the streetcar to come home. My father would come home later, and I would inform him that I had made my way home on my own, thank you very much, because I was a big girl. I was seven.

Joyce pointed out that children's freedom to travel was extensive, and no one worried about them. Children got on trolleys and buses without hesitation. Her only requirement was that she needed to be home by dark.

As I got a little older, my friends and I would initiate more trips. We would go downtown to the Denver Theater to see a play, taking our lunch with us, then maybe stay to see a double feature. Then someone would pick us up or we would take the streetcar home. All that fun would occupy us from the morning until late into the afternoon. The streetcars were clean, convenient and always had people on them.

For a child, the streetcars allowed Joyce to make Denver her oyster of enjoyment. She took school trips to the symphony, practiced ballet downtown at the Tabor Theater and studied creative dramatics at the University of Denver, getting ice cream at the corner shop along the way. Any ice cream she didn't have the stomach to finish she could eat on the trolley, for food was allowed on board.

Our parents had told us what parts of town to avoid, like some of the theaters downtown, so we avoided them and kept on going. It was freedom, and that was fun! Of course, there were some things that girls did not do. The boys liked to pull the cord down so that the streetcar lost power. Girls never did that, of course.

When asked about the transition from streetcars to buses, Joyce responded that it was something out of the movie *Back to the Future.*

We were happy kids, too dumb to know what was going on around us. The change from one to the other was just something that you accepted. We did not think about it. The streetcar came, and later the bus came, and you got where you were going. So, no one that I remember was sad to see the streetcar depart for good.

Joyce was thirteen when the final streetcars ambled along Denver's streets in 1950.

Now, living in Capitol Hill, Joyce gets around via bus. She has taken a few trips for fun on the Light Rail train, but living so close to downtown, it is not a transit mode that aids her overmuch. Still, the experience of being on the train has caused her to reexamine the advantage of having rail-based transit.

I have enjoyed taking the Light Rail; I've always been a fan of public transit. Now, when I think back on those days and how carefree I was with the streetcar, I am very sad that they were removed. I think part of it was change just for change's sake, which I don't think is valid. I am glad we are moving back toward having a mix of ways to get around Denver. The poor have always been left out of so many considerations, and transit gives everyone an option, it gives everyone access. My family and I lived in a place without public transportation for a while, and believe me you notice it when it's not there! Denver's going to do great!

Judith W. was not as free to roam as Joyce was, but the streetcar was no less exciting for her. She grew up on South Franklin Street, just north of Washington Park, and rode the Number 5 streetcar, first with her mother and later on her own. Riding the streetcar was a routine event, but not without moments of interest.

Mr. Delohery, who lived across the street from us, owned a tavern on South Broadway, and he would take the Number 5 streetcar every morning. We all boarded at Dakota and Franklin. If Mr. D. happened to ride the same car, he would pay all the fares for all the ladies and children boarding with him. He would say it was because we were so pretty or he liked the color of our dress, that sort of thing. He was a charming Irish man and passed away a short while after the streetcars stopped running.

When summer arrived, and school relinquished its hold on Judith's schedule, she would ride the streetcar to get to various activities, wearing clothing suited to active summertime pursuits. Wearing shorts or skirts did have one consequence for young ladies riding the streetcar, however: upon leaving the streetcar, the pattern of the wicker seats would be firmly impressed in the backs of one's legs.

In late summer, when we had grown bored with summer vacation, we would sit on the curb and watch the late afternoon streetcar, carrying more passengers at this time of day, make the sharp, noisy turn from Alameda to Franklin. There would usually be a lot of screeching of metal on metal as the heavy car made the turn, and crackling of electricity, between the trolley and overhead wire. On occasion—not often—the streetcar would go off the track, or the trolley would disconnect from the overhead wire. This would necessitate a service crew coming to the scene to set things right and, like most kids, we would consider that to be a pretty interesting way for the afternoon to end! Remember: we didn't have television until 1952 and certainly no computer games.

An aunt visiting from Pennsylvania in 1948 asked the family in vexation how in the world they could sleep at night with the noisy streetcar going by, ringing its bell at the corner. After a moment of consideration, they all agreed that they were so accustomed to it that they didn't even notice the sounds.

The streetcar really helped our family because my father traveled, working as a salesman throughout a wide territory. My mother and I had no other means of transportation during his absence, so we regarded living on the Number 5 streetcar line a very fortunate thing!

The streetcar took the family to the post office, Safeway or Miller's Supermarket, to music lessons, doctor's appointments, church and the movies.

The movies were especially wonderful. We could go to the movies at either the Alameda Theater, at Alameda and Pearl, the Park Theater, on South Gaylord, the Mayan, on Broadway, and even the Webber Theater on South Broadway. Of course, it presented a different kind of entertainment in those days than does Kitty's South today!

Born in 1931 and growing up on Fourth between Race and Vine, near the Country Club and Cherry Creek, Mary Louise M. left for college just before the streetcars exited Denver as well. All the same, the years prior to college have left indelible impressions of getting around town. Moreover, she has some memories of the streetcar conductors themselves.

We rode the Numbers 4 and 6, starting my education at Bromwell Elementary and then going to Kent Denver, which was in Capitol Hill then.

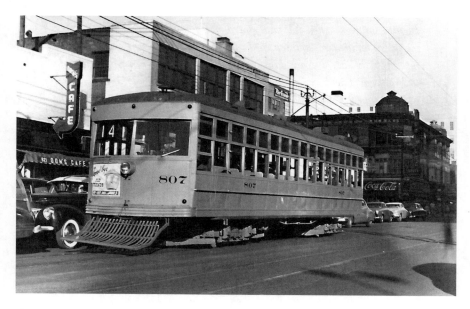

Though warmth could be supplied to the streetcars via electric heaters, air conditioning was more problematic. The riders on this East Colfax streetcar on closing day, June 3, have opened the windows to catch some cool afternoon air. *RTD*.

I walked to Sixth Avenue and transferred at Broadway, riding with other people but without my parents. I used tokens or coins to pay. I remember how wonderful the streetcars were in the winter, because they were always nice and warm when it was cold outside. Sometimes coming home they were crowded, but the seats were comfortable, and they were warm! I loved listening to the fare boxes. As the change fell down into them, it was a tinkling music. There were people to watch and advertisements above to read. In some parts of town there were buses going in to replace the streetcars even before I went off to Boulder for school. I remember being sad to see the streetcars go, because they were very appealing, but the buses were clean and spiffy.

Sometimes, before coming home from school, Mary Louise would stop by the drugstore to get a candy bar. She would eat it on the streetcars, and all evidence of her snack would be long gone before she got home…or so she thought!

My mother told me I shouldn't be buying such things because I would get fat. She couldn't see me eating on the streetcar, so how had she known I was eating candy bars? I had thought a warm streetcar and some chocolate was perfection itself.

When the family needed to go farther afield, such as Elitch Gardens, they took the car. For her father's daily commute to the Republic Building (corner of Sixteenth Street and Tremont) and general travel to and from downtown, it was the streetcar that got them there.

Everyone in my family took the streetcar, but I was really the one who used it the most. It gave me the freedom to get out! There was a painted spot on the roadway where you were supposed to stand for the streetcar to pick you up, and cars were not supposed to drive there. When you wanted to get off the streetcar, you pulled a cord. A buzzer would sound, and the conductor would stop for you. That all sounds very congenial, but the conductors were really not very nice sometimes. They were not supposed to fraternize with the passengers at all, so they tended to be very antisocial. I didn't like them glaring at me.

Joanne L. did not attend one of the Denver Public Schools; she attended St. Mary's Academy, which used to be located at 1480 Pennsylvania Street, in Denver's Capitol Hill neighborhood.

We lived in what is today Cherry Hills Village, a long way south from my father's work downtown and from my school. During my four years at St. Mary's Academy, from 1944 until 1948, my father would drive to work each day, dropping me off at school on the way. When the school day was done, I would catch the streetcar at Colfax and Pennsylvania, then transfer at Downing to head south to Cherry Hills Village. I came home that way all four years. It was a great time on the streetcar. They were warm in the winter, which was nice. They were not air conditioned, which meant they could get quite hot in the nicer months, and there were many students on the streetcar with me. Everyone rode the streetcar, all ages, and I felt very safe. Eventually St. Mary's moved closer to where we lived, so my younger sisters didn't take the streetcar for their entire high school experience, as I did, so I was lucky.

Jamie M., who now lives in Palm Beach Gardens, Florida, shared her streetcar memories with her children. When one of those children, now grown, found out that memories from that time period were being gathered and told his mother, she eagerly compiled a set to be shared.

The streetcars were wonderful, as they gave a young girl a brilliant taste of being independent and seeing the big city. It helped me develop a sense of curiosity. We lived in Pueblo, but I had a reason to go to Denver. My mother and father took this trip with me for the first time to instruct and show me the way and the precautions to take. Early almost every Saturday morning, from the summer of 1944 through the spring of 1947, I would ride the Pueblo streetcar to the train station, then take the train to Denver, which was a journey of about an hour and a half. I would then disembark at Union Station in Denver. I got to do all this for free because my father was a chief dispatcher for the Denver and Rio Grande Railroad. I had a free pass, so I made use of it to go to Denver. Why? I was taking flute lessons! My teacher was Mr. DeSouse, who was the first flutist with the Denver Symphony.

Starting the summer before her freshman year at Pueblo Centennial High School, the experience was always memorable.

I caught a streetcar near Union Station. The streetcar headed right up Seventeenth Street, through all the buildings and bustle, then out beyond East High School. I don't remember the street now, but it was near City Park. I got off the streetcar and walked a block and a half to Mr. DeSouse's house for my lesson. I remember thinking that going over the streetcar tracks must be very bumpy for the cars. The streetcar had a clanging bell, which would ring when we approached a scheduled stop and the conductor would call out the street name in a resonant voice.

In almost three years of taking flute lessons one hundred miles from her home, Jamie only had one experience when the schedule did not work out right.

My mother and father always told me that I was NEVER to accept an automobile ride from anyone, but one day the schedule was really off because it was so snowy. I felt so cold and was just standing there because I had missed my streetcar back to Union Station. I was mortified, trying to determine what to do. This very nice looking couple offered me a ride because of the cold. I was lucky that they were as nice as they looked. They dropped me off downtown, which is where they were going.

Jamie was a very responsible teenager and had a wide menu of choices for other diversions while in Denver.

82

My train did not leave for Pueblo until 4:30 or so. That got me home in time for dinner or, as sometimes happened later in high school, a date. Since my flute lesson was finished before lunch, I would have time to go to the Museum of Natural History [today's Denver Museum of Nature and Science] *in City Park or take the trolley downtown and take in a movie. My parents told me I should never get off the trolley at Larimer Street, and I didn't! It was Skid Row then, with all the drunks and homeless making the street their hangout. My, how it has changed! Even with avoiding one street, the experiences the streetcar allowed me in Denver were wonderful!*

Betty B. also grew up in another part of the state but had the good fortune to experience Denver in the full flush of its transit boom.

I lived in Glenwood Springs from 1937 to 1946 and coming to the big city of Denver was a real treat. My father, Richard, was a deputy collector for the Internal Revenue Service. He was stationed in Glenwood Springs and made several trips to the "head office" in Denver for meetings. On occasion, my mother and I were able to come along. In Denver, we stayed at the Savoy Hotel. While Dad attended his business meetings, my mother and I would take the streetcar all the way out to the Museum of Natural History. What an exciting ride for a little girl from a little town! We would spend the day in this wonderland. My favorites were the huge dinosaur and the display of the North American animals. When we came back to the hotel, Dad would take us out to dinner at the Blue Parrot Restaurant on Broadway, where we were greeted at the door by the big blue parrot in his glass cage. On special evenings we would take the streetcar to the beautiful Elitch Gardens to attend a play in the famous old playhouse. After the play, we walked across to the outdoor ballroom, where my parents glided around the floor to the big band sounds. Then, to end the evening perfectly, another ride on the streetcar! Coming to Denver was a delight!

Dorine G., who attended Byers Junior High School in 1945–46, recalled the experience of being on the streetcar with significantly less delight than many of her contemporaries.

The boys loved to pull the cord down from the overhead wire, which stopped the trolley dead. The driver either put it back or said we would not move until the person who had taken it off put it back on! We would sit there until the next streetcar came along. The next driver would be mad to find a streetcar in his way, and he would put it on so both could continue. I often got off in the streetcar in the winter to walk home, on South Gaylord, because the streetcars were always so hot. It made me sick!

Others, such as Patricia V., echo Dorine's mixed reviews.

You would enter the streetcar at the center with a conductor facing you to have you pay your fare. He then signaled the motorman in front, and the car would go. You could sit ahead or behind. The conductors wore uniforms and caps, like the police or milkmen. As kids, we did not ask out parents to take us anywhere and rode all over the Denver area, often by ourselves. We took Charlie, the family dog, with us and had to pay adult fare for him as he preferred a window seat! I rode the Number 8, which I caught at Pearl and Buchtel Boulevard. People today often discuss the charm of the streetcars, but there was a downside. They were cold in the winter, since the heat ran under the seats, and they were hot in the summer. The windows were hard to open and close, and there were those who did not care what others preferred; they would open or close the windows and make the rest of us suffer. Sometimes we would be downtown and need to head home about rush hour. We would walk closer to the Loop because the streetcars filled up rapidly, with people even standing in the aisle. They were crammed as closely as possible, with the handle on the back of the seat to hold on to and no such thing as a smooth start or stop. It was not a feat for sissies! Men were great at giving up seats for the ladies, though. Once the car was full, it did not stop for additional passengers. After dark, with so many people standing so no one could see where the streetcar had reached, the conductor would have to call out the upcoming street. You would descend from the back door after pulling the cord to sound the buzzer. The streetcars were noisy, smelly and hot, but Charlie enjoyed the ride!

For many people, the experience of riding the streetcar was shared by folks of every generation, from parents to grandparents and farther back. One's perception of the ride could depend a great deal on whether you were aboard as a passenger or as an employee. As an example of this, Linda R.'s memories of the streetcar are happier than those of her grandfather.

The streetcars had what were called "cow catchers" on the fronts and many lives were saved when someone walked in front of the trolley and just got tossed aside by the catchers with only minor injuries. I would watch the pattern of bricks and rails and other things in the road as we traveled. My brother was more interested in watching the sparks fly when they crossed wires at the intersection. My grandfather, who was a conductor for the Tramway and drove many years, said he was supposed to stop every other block. Once, a lady wanted off in between and my grandfather told her no, so she jumped off and was killed. My grandfather lost his job because of that.

Others have similarly oppositional impressions. Roberta B., who lived at Forty-fifth Avenue and Yates Street, nearly had a streetcar cost her the chance of making any memories at all.

We lived near a road called Short Yates and the streetcar came down that road before jogging onto Yates right at our corner. One evening a streetcar jumped the tracks and would have landed in our living room if we had not had a high cement step in front of the house. The step stopped the streetcar's momentum and saved us. After everything came to a stop, my grandfather was certain that the overhead power lines had fallen, so he would not let us go outside until help came. No one was hurt. Most of the time, however, the streetcar was a great thing. I would ride home from Alcott Elementary and sing as the car swayed on the curves. What a great memory!

Even those on the streetcar had to be aware of the potential for danger, as Mary C. relates.

The dangerous part was getting on and off the streetcar. The tracks were in the middle of the street, so we had to watch for cars and some did not stop for us. It was a noisy ride, especially if the windows were open on a hot day, but it was also grand to go downtown to shop or see a movie.

Jennie S.'s family would come to Denver from Loveland for any major shopping. As a child of five, Denver was as exhilarating as it was frightening.

I always stayed close to Momma! The streetcars were such a bright yellow and once you were aboard, they would jerk to a start very alarmingly. I was afraid of downtown Denver, but my father had a business which brought him into the city from time to time, and my Momma and I would come to shop while he did business things. We went to Grant's Department Store and D&F. My father's business had suppliers on Market and Larimer, but we could watch those creepy, disintegrating buildings go by from the safety of those splendid yellow streetcars!

Wilma T. also experienced the streetcars at a very young age.

When I was five and under, I used to ride the Number 5 streetcar into downtown Denver. We lived at South Josephine Street and Arizona Avenue. I remember the streetcar being a dirty mustard yellow. Climbing up onto the streetcar benches was always a major effort for me. They had metal frames and not much padding, but I loved to sit where I could see the overhead attachments pivot as we turned corners. The wires and connectors would spark occasionally, especially on the turns. I always wanted to see that and was so disappointed when my brother got the window seat! We did not ride it often, but when we did it was for something special. We would go shopping and make a whole day of it. On the streetcar ride home I would just sleep because I was so tired.

Born at St. Luke's Hospital in 1924, Shirley G. was raised by her paternal grandparents, who lived at Twenty-eighth and Josephine. She and her family rode the Number 28 because nobody had an automobile. Her perceptions, shaped by her grandmother's words, are just as vivid today as when she was a little girl.

As we rode along, my grandmother would talk about everything we were passing. I just sat and listened to my grandmother as she talked about buildings, describing them as we went by, and even examined each and every tree and what was happening in it. I might as well have been a blind person, my grandmother's descriptions were so clear. My grandmother would say to me, "Shirley, we need to get out." That was her term, the announcement that we were going to go and have an adventure. The streetcar was our way of having it, our way of getting there. She would always make it quite dramatic, sweeping into the room and saying "We're going to take a trip today," or something to that effect. We dressed up, so that we looked nice. We got on the streetcar and our big day began.

The family did not have enough money to do many shopping trips, but they would occasionally get the money together for a movie or a visit to an amusement park. Theaters like the Victory, the Rialto and the Tabor were ones Shirley knew well, though nearby Bauer's Candies was a place they

Boarding a streetcar or interurban car was a passport to adventure, whatever a person's age. *RTD.*

could not afford to enter, and as a child she always imagined it as some kind of heaven. These experiences were not restricted to weekends, either; sometimes, to avoid the crowds, Shirley's grandmother would take her out on a school day, since true adventures cannot be limited to any particular day of the week.

> *We could never even dream of going through the door* [of Bauer's]. *We would go by it, nothing more. This was long before the Cherry Creek shopping area was even heard of, so we would walk around downtown and just look at all of it. By the time I entered sixth grade at Columbine Elementary, I had just shot up in height. I was 5'8" and growing like a weed. Since paying the fare was that much more money, my grandmother would sometimes say to me, "Shirley, you have got to scrunch down so you look young." I would scrunch down and get on for free. I don't think it really fooled the driver, but he would usually be nice and let me on all the same.*

According to Shirley, everyone rode the streetcar. It was a great way for people of all types to mix. The cars offered large windows so that everyone could have a good view. The experience of growing up without a car is one

Since streetcars were tracked along the center of streets rather than the edges, riders had to worry about cars zipping around the streetcar when it stopped so people could board or disembark. *CRM.*

that Shirley has taken to its fullest conclusion: even during adult years when she lived in Boston, New York City and San Jose, California, Shirley has never owned a car.

> *Sometimes our home was quite cold, so getting into a nice warm streetcar was bliss. People in those days were used to adapting and making do. No one assumed the temperature would be just right, no matter what.*

In 1950, when buses replaced streetcars completely, Shirley was living in the Swansea neighborhood of Denver. By this time a mother in her own right, she would gather her children and hop on one of the many buses in the area.

> *We would ride to the Tabor, just on the bus instead of the trolley, and have ourselves an outing! My husband made a good living, so I could take the children to all the places I had never gotten to go as a child. We didn't just look in the windows at Bauer's. We went in and ate! For all that, I barely remember the buses themselves. Riding the streetcars was so much more interesting than riding any bus. Buses can't hold a candle to a streetcar.*

The streetcars gave a young girl without a lot of financial freedom the chance to spread her wings all over Denver, a joyous familiarity she would later share with all her children. This was one of the many possibilities offered by the streetcar.

For Janene L., she *did* take the freedom to spread one's wings to a bit of an extreme, though at least it ended well.

> *I loved going out to eat, and the streetcar is how we got to places with great food. I remember that there were delicious doughnuts and freshly made taffy at the Loop Market. There were so many tasty things out there, but that ended up getting me into trouble, and the streetcar helped me in my mischief. We lived at Sixth and Marion and my mother, Virginia, worked at Eddie Bohn's Pig 'N Whistle* [a famous barbeque restaurant on West Colfax just east of Sheridan; closed in 1991, the building burned down in 2010]. *Eddie had a soft spot for my mother because she was a nice lady and a great worker. My grandmother would take us to the restaurant quite a bit, to eat and say hello to my mother during her shift. We always took the streetcar to get there. Well, one day I found a nickel on the street. I was hungry and certainly knew the way, having done it so many times with my grandmother, so I rode all the way to the restaurant (a distance of about five miles). I loved that restaurant. It had decorations in the basement showing the Three Little Pigs, the Big Bad Wolf and other themes dealing with barbeque. My mother wasn't working that day, so when I got there I was not only alone, but there was also no one there to see. Eddie asked me where my mother and grandmother were, and I replied I wanted a steak for my lunch and had come on my own. Money didn't quite occur to me, and I had used my nickel to cover the fare. Well, I got my steak. Meanwhile, Eddie called my mother. She showed up a short while later. When she offered to pay for the lunch I had enjoyed, Eddie just smiled and told her that Jack Dempsey, the famous boxer, had paid for my meal. I don't think that's true, but Eddie was nice that way. Anyway, we got back on the streetcar and headed home. By the time we got there, much of my mother's anger had cooled. She thought it kind of funny, her little lady all grown up and crossing town for a steak dinner. I still got a spanking, but it was not as bad as it could have been.*

Though Clarence E.'s memories have been softened to a nostalgic point by time, he remembers his streetcar experiences with quite mixed reviews.

> *We took the streetcar for school and to visit family. I rode by myself sometimes, even at seven years of age. I was not scared. The cars were*

This interior view shows the fare box, to the right of the operator, and the rattan seats that were said to "pinch" some riders. A fare box like the one shown here is currently undergoing conservation at the Aurora History Museum and will be displayed when its parent streetcar is opened to the public. *RTD.*

always cold and drafty and had wicker seats that would pinch you. As you went along the streets, the streetcar would rock back and forth, and the seats would pinch something awful. It was not a comfortable ride, but what did you expect in those days? We were kids and didn't know any better. If you can't compare it to anything else, you don't know. It was as comfortable as anything else. All the same, I miss the streetcar now. For me, riding the streetcar always had a mystique; it was fun to do. It was like a ride at Elitch's. When they put the buses in it was like riding a bus…nothing special at all.

Diane S., though too young to remember the streetcar at all, having been born in 1948, has a long connection to it through her family.

My mother, Elaine, took the streetcar everywhere as most people did. Most of the time it was normal and fine, but she related a couple of stories to me about how the olden days still had their share of problems. People want to think that everything was great back then, but I think it's just that people didn't talk about bad things. My mother and her sister got off the streetcar to go to the Jewell Theater on Broadway. They'd barely stepped away from the streetcar when a man in an overcoat flashed them; they screamed and ran up the road. Toward the end of high school, she worked downtown at Ward's. She always came in and out of downtown on the same car, so she was a familiar face to the conductors, even if they didn't necessarily know her name. My mother's family lived in South Denver, near the end of the line. One night, when she was coming home from work, everyone had gotten off the streetcar along the way except one man. She was sitting up front by the conductor. When she got to her stop and stood up to get off, the guy in the back stood up too. The conductor, in a low and urgent voice, told her to sit back down. Since she had been sitting right next to him, she sat back down, though she did not understand what was happening. When she sat back down, the guy in the back sat back down as well. The conductor went to the next stop and then he only opened the door in the front so Mom could get off. He kept the back door closed. He told her, "I am going to watch you run up to the next corner. I will watch until I can give you enough time to get a head start." He could tell the man in the back of the streetcar was up to no good.

Not all Diane's connections to Denver's transit history are so frightening, however. Her mother's father, C.J., often told her stories about *his* father, Edwin. Edwin had been a conductor on the Cherrelyn Horsecar, in Englewood.

My grandfather was always proud of the fact that his father had been part of such an interesting aspect of our history. He would tell the story to anyone and everyone. At the end of World War I, he was in New York City and stopped in a barber shop to get a trim before he came to Denver. Above the barber chairs was a large, framed picture of the Cherrelyn, in Denver. When the barber noticed my grandfather looking at the picture, he asked 'That's out in Colorado. The horse pulls the car up the hill and then rides down. Have you heard about it?' My grandfather laughed and answered, 'Heard about it? The conductor in the picture is my father!'

For the Turners, the memories of riding the streetcar have a great impact; their father, Harry Turner, was an employee of the Denver Tramway Corporation for many years and drove one of the vehicles. Peggy, Twila and Gene Turner all offered insights into how the streetcar touched their family.

Twila's memories of her family's association are not numerous but have a strength often associated with childhood recollections based on emotion rather than the play of events.

Harry Turner poses in his uniform as an operator for the Denver Tramway Corporation. On the back of the picture were written the words, "Here's the old boy. He isn't any good, is he?" Though not visible in the picture, motormen and conductors had a badge that indicated their seniority number; this would have been on their hats. *Turner Family collection.*

Harry Turner, in his tramway operator uniform, posed with his wife, Celia, for this picture. Harry enjoyed his work very much and shared his pride with his children, frequently taking them on his streetcar so they could enjoy some extra time together. *Turner Family Collection.*

My father was very proud to wear the uniform and hat; it was a big job for him. I didn't know it at the time, but it was quite a career opportunity for him. He'd worked smaller jobs before, as an auto mechanic, doing road construction with the Works Progress Administration, but no job that could be a profession. I remember as a young girl catching a ride on his trolley and riding to the end of the route and back again, just to be with him.

Peggy's memories were similar.

I was SO proud of my father as a conductor. I was a young girl, just barely in school, but I was just thrilled to sit in the center-facing seat where I could watch Dad as he worked with the customers that got on and off the streetcar. The gentle, rolling movement of the car actually felt great and always brought a smile. I remember a lot of smiles from both my father and the customers. Everyone who got on and off the streetcar seemed to have time to visit with Dad, who was quite a social individual. Daddy loved his job. I knew it then, and I heard it from my mother in later years too.

Peggy felt the era of the streetcar was a grand time for Denver. People were easier and friendlier in their transactions. The streetcar was "where we connected with each other." People could get anywhere with the streetcar, Peggy remembers, including the family home in the Barnum neighborhood of Denver.

Gene Turner expanded on his sisters' sentiments.

We got free rides because our father was a conductor. My brothers and sisters would sometimes take turns riding with Dad just to be with him. Only one at a time, so my father didn't have to take too much attention away from his work. It was always exciting to ride the streetcar. My father was really good at getting unruly people off the streetcar, and he could almost always do it by talking rather than by force. The streetcars were cold in the winter, OK in the summer, but we didn't care; we were kids. We didn't know any better. As for Dad, he enjoyed his job. He was very personable. After he had been on his route for a short time, he knew everyone by first name. He would greet them and tell folks all the news. If they were tourists, he would point out nice places to visit.

Being an energetic boy, Gene sometimes had fun with the streetcars as other boys did. The cord between the streetcar and the overhead wire held a great deal of tension and could, at certain times, be pulled down quite readily. Gene declared he could do the deed pretty quickly, which naturally brought the streetcar to a dead stop. The chaos was always amusing to watch, though Gene carefully made clear that he never did this to his father's streetcar. Gene concluded his recollections with a sad memory concerning his father, however.

> *Unfortunately, Dad ended up losing his job at the Tramway. He was on his route late at night, and snow was everywhere. He was working on his transfers and not paying complete attention. Maybe he hit the curve too fast or it was extra slippery because of the snow, but he tipped the streetcar over onto its side. No one was on board, and he was not hurt himself, but it damaged the vehicle, so he lost his job over that. I know he was devastated and always regretted losing a job where he had such pride.*

In autumn of 2002, the *Alumni Confederate*, a newsletter for the graduates of South High School, asked for memories of riding the interurban trolleys. The newsletter opens with some explanatory text.

> *During the first half of the twentieth century, Denver had an excellent "Light Rail System." With the advent of the automobile age* [however], *which provided more personal freedom of mobility, the system was dismantled and the emphasis was placed on building public highways.*

Some South High School students obligingly offered memories. One alumnus recalled riding the interurban trolley to Golden to attend classes at the School of Mines. Students there referred to the trolley as "the Golden Goose."

> *The trolleys used in interurban service were larger than the streetcars used in town. The route was about thirteen miles and punctuated with quaint names for some of the stops: Bee Hive, Morningside, Treatdale, Wide Acres and Jack Rabbit Crossing.*

Darrell P. shared some of his memories. "I rode [the interurban] from downtown Denver, the old Loop Market, to go fishing in Clear Creek. The thing that impressed me the most about riding it was when the motorman got it cranked up to its top speed, somewhere in what is now western Lakewood. The car would start rocking back and forth and you would wonder if it was going to jump off the track. It never did, of course."

REMARKABLE REMARKS

MISS ANDERSON: Staying out nights has become an annual occurrence.

MISS BERGER: Forty-five minutes, seventh hour.

MRS. BUCK: The next best thing to being a man is having one.

MISS CONINE: Many a pupil has failed because he couldn't draw his breath.

MR. CURTIS: It's an ancient and honorable sport.

MRS. EVANS: I missed the seven and the eight was late.

MISS FORD: Take this slip to the office and have it okehed.

MISS GARDINER: It is possible by superimposing the fourth dimension on the theory of limits to solve the Eternal Triangle.

MR. GLENS: By applying the principles of Watt and Stevenson to gas engines we discover that, in general, when the gas tank is empty, the engine stops.

MR. HANFL: By a strict adherence to the principles of osmosis, metabolism, and photosynthesis it is possible to raise the median production of a flock of white leghorns three-fourths of an egg per day.

MISS HARVEY: The ouija board says I'm to be kidnapped. Oh! I'm so excited I just can't wait!

MR. HILL: Isn't it disgusting—Father is sick, and the deer season is opening.

MR. KENYON: The principal's all right when he functions.

MISS KIMBALL: My dear children; a Russian is a Red because he hasn't.

MISS MARKUSEN: Get 'em young; treat 'em rough; tell 'em nothing and scare 'em to death.

MISS MEANY: The Spanish language is doubly beneficial inasmuch as it exercises all the muscles of the body.

MISS MORRISON: When you talk you get up and stand on both feet.

MISS MITCHELL: Let us get thru chewing.

MRS. PRESTON: Gallia est omnis divisa in partes tres.

MISS RUDOLPH: If Julius Caesar had read Burke's Conciliation Milton would have written major instead of minor poems. Remember the curse of the minimum.

MISS SCHEIDT: One's education in French is not complete until he has been to France and heard the Pheasants sing the Mayonaisse.

MISS SCHODER: Garcon, aimez-vous la langue Francaise tres bien?

MR. TURNER: When the sun comes down and the moon goes up.

MR. UTTERBACK: You owe me $1.15.

MR. CORY: Who wrote this excuse?

The teachers of South High School were asked to relate the most memorable excuses they had received that year. No doubt the students believed tardiness was more excusable when the delay was due to the streetcar. Mrs. Evans evidently did not think so. The nearby streetcars 7 and 8 would have taken many students to and from South. *South High School.*

In a smattering of pictures from the year, we find a group of streetcar operators at the doorway of their vehicle in the image at the top of the page. Were they South High School alum who now worked on the streetcars? We may never know, but we can certainly hope that they were not letting high school students drive! *South High School.*

You don't love me anymore

Hessie and Tessie

No two ways about it

Brrt!

Field trip to the zoo

9 out of 10 eat Corn Flakes.

Scrambled eggs

Our inhuman relations

Melon-Collie

Even girls got in on the streetcar act at South High School. In the image at the upper right, a young lady, perhaps wearing the cap of a relative, tries her hand at an imaginary drive along the streetcar tracks. *South High School.*

The interurban cars did more than just carry people; they also carried items. In this image, we see that stacks of newspapers have been brought to distant Arvada, no doubt to appear on newsstand shelves throughout the area a short time later.

Perhaps decked out for an exciting day in downtown Denver, these ladies are boarding an interurban car at Clear Creek Junction. There are no ramps for handicapped access anywhere to be seen. Accessibility is one of the ways in which the modern system is an improvement on its predecessor. *RTD.*

Lakeside Amusement Park, also known as the White City, had streetcar access to its front doors. In addition to allowing park-goers young and old to reach the park, it allowed them respite on the way home to nurse their bruises from all the wild rides. *RTD.*

Bob P. shared some of these perceptions. "I am sure [everyone who rode the interurban would] remark about the wild ride. Though it had a wider gauge track than the similar streetcars, its ride was so fast and the roadbed so uneven we were sure the lurching would result in our being flung, spinning, tumbling far off the tracks. It was then that I first associated the words MORTALITY and ME. Anyway, it was cheaper than the rides at Elitch's or Lakeside!"

Additional students recount the trip as being more placid, more intent on the destination itself. Golden offered camping, hiking, fishing and other recreational opportunities. The interurban was greatly appreciated by everyone for connecting Denver and Golden so reliably and efficiently, even if the vehicles rocked in getting there!

In the 1920s, local newspapers would print the detailed list of everything going on with the Denver Tramway, such as the latest derailments, delays and their causes. This is how people learned what was going on with this vital aspect of the community's function. Pamphlets such as *As-You-Go*, printed from the 1930s until the early 1950s, informed those who wanted to read something on their journey. The tramway was much debated in the newspapers and among politicians and citizens, and it stood as an elementary aspect of many people's lives before being routed so thoroughly by the car. All the same, there were many aspects of the company's function that were not known to the general public. There are some who have gathered these minute traces, studiously piecing them together to provide a richer and deeper picture of a business that long shaped Denver. These have not been casual students of streetcar history. These have been historians-as-soldiers, standing at the vanguard of the fray, fighting to keep every precious fragment from being lost to the foe of time, which obscures more and more with each tick of the clock. Most of them have been lost to us. Among those still seeking the rails of yesteryear is Kenton Forrest. Though he never actually saw a streetcar function on Denver's streets, there are few who have ever known the system's operation as well.

When we moved to Denver, I attended Gust Elementary. I would frequently see the Number 18 bus, which terminated across the street, when I got out of school each day. When my parents and I were out in the car, I would see other buses. I noticed they had different numbers, showed up in different places. I wanted to figure out the pattern, so I got a notebook and began noting each bus I saw, where it was, when and what route number.

The bus system was like ours in many ways, being carried on tires and fueled by gasoline, but there were some significant differences as well. In those days, there were no schedules accessible to the public. Though snippets of schedules might appear in the *As-You-Go* pamphlet, the general practice was to head outside and simply wait. You knew a streetcar would come by, but unless you were a frequent rider and knew the general schedule, you had no way of knowing when precisely.

Though his meticulous note-taking of bus service around the neighborhood was not something he shared with his classmates, he did share other more prosaic pursuits of childhood.

When I got to high school, I started taking the buses downtown. I could get some lunch, watch a movie at the Paramount and still have money to come home. That was when it was seven and a half cents, the student rate. I did that kind of day out all the time. I didn't yet know about the kind of strict schedules governing the bus operators, schedules we didn't have access to in the public. Streetcar conductors and then, later, bus operators had schedules they were expected to keep, even down to the half minute.

Unless there was a fire or some kind of blockage of the route, you were to be on time. Otherwise, you would "be on the carpet." That was not a good thing. I didn't know that then, of course. I mostly just took the buses to get places and kept my notebook. While I was riding, though, I began talking to the operators. I got to know Howard Rank, who was hired just after the streetcar strike. He ran the Number 55 bus. When I was coming home from high school many nights I would ride with Walt Byers. He liked for me to be along with him on his route, because if someone else was on the bus then no one would rob him. Walt told me lots of stories about working for the Tramway Corporation.

Walt Byers shared a story that would help Kenton in his own thirty-year-long career as a middle school science teacher. Walt operated a school tripper from West High School into downtown Denver, transporting lots of kids. The kids would occasionally open the back windows, which offered ready access to the cord that connected to the streetcar's power supply overhead. The mischief-makers would pull the cord, severing the connection. This would normally get a rise from the streetcar operator, who then had to go through the laborious process of reattaching streetcar to overhead wire. Walt had a different answer, however.

He would close the controller arm for the vehicle, get out a book and start to read. The kids would get mad and run around, but he just sat there implacable. Finally the kids concluded that Walt was no fun and, rather than keep sitting there indefinitely, they would reattach the cord themselves. Once the motor began, Walt could hear it right away. He would put his book away and resume his route as if nothing had happened. He never had any problem controlling the kids.

Upon graduating from West High School, Kenton went to school at Colorado State College in Greeley, getting a degree to teach science. During breaks from classes and work, he delved ever more deeply into the working of the Denver Tramway Corporation. Hired immediately out of college to work at Dunstan Middle School in Jefferson County, he expanded his research without ever really interlacing the two elements of his life. During the weekdays, he was a science teacher. Evenings and weekends, and especially during summer vacation, he was a miner digging into the fertile history of Denver transit.

I began to talk to everyone. Henry Couperus got me started. [Mr. Couperus was a noted historian on the city's transit history and published *History of Denver Tramway Routes.*] *I worked with him to translate his information on streetcar routes into maps. I did the number crunching for all the routes, some of which changed a lot and some barely at all. I got to know people in the transit union. I figured out how to read headway sheets* [for scheduling]. *This was all before the computer. It was done by hand. I knew who was on what route and when. One fellow, for example, was Archie Campbell. He had to be to the car barn each day by 4:00 a.m. He went to North Denver to bring all the other operators to the car barn as well. They could then go to work. Meanwhile, Archie did two more trips, on the Number 13, before going home. He had to get to bed early because he didn't get up at 4:00; he had to be to work by then!*

Kenton began to seek out and interview retired tramway conductors, people in the maintenance shop, schedulers and anyone else at the tramway who would talk to him. In return for his enthusiasm, he got pictures, rule books (some dating back to the days of the cable car) and more, all in an effort to fill in the picture of mass transit in Denver. Some of the people were in nursing homes, some with their minds failing, but Kenton would work with them patiently to gather their tales and impressions. His work removed some of the gaps, but not all. The questions would seem murky and venial to most people, but to those whose mission is the tramway, they were beguiling.

During his summer vacations and as many times as he could during the school year, Kenton would go to the accounting department. They would give him boxes of stuff. Garage clerks would hand him piles as well, all their daily operations in and out of the car barn. Kenton could have filled whole houses with it all, so he had to pick some of it for his records and throw the rest away.

I went all year and everyone knew me, from the high powers-that-be in the offices to the workers in the garages. One of the garage clerks was Joe Guliani, who did the forms to determine which buses went out the next morning and in which order. They had to leave in just the right way or there would be pandemonium. Doing it all by hand, long before computers, Joe could get the ordering done in no time at all. Each driver had a mailbox, with announcements, daily assignments, route changes and the like, as well as his change. He would get that when he came in the next day. The best thing they ever did was go to exact fare...saved the drivers a lot of trouble.

This car barn at Thirty-fifth and Gilpin still stands today, though no longer serving a transit function. In the distance to the right, the roofline of today's Wyatt-Edison Charter School may be seen. This was one of the facilities where operators picked up their streetcars for their daily runs. *CRM.*

This is the end of Route 4, which would be about a few blocks east of Colorado Boulevard at about First. The conductor (on ground) is Howard Rank and the motorman is A.R. Phillips. Notice the coin changer that Mr. Rank wears at his waist. Attached to the wearer like a harness, these could get heavy! *Lakewood Heritage Center.*

Kenton made sure that he and his friends rode any route that was being discontinued as well, such as the old Number 31, which used to run as a circulator from Westminster to Regis University and back. This route was discontinued in 1969.

Joe Guliani, when he found out that we were going to be taking that last bus, arranged for the flagship bus of the fleet, the Number 119, to be sent out that day. It was a very large bus, far larger than the driver was accustomed to because the route was just a little circulator. The driver was startled, but took his moment in the spotlight well.

I also rode the high rail car when they were doing the abandonment of the line from Prospect Junction to the Federal Center, in the late '60s. This was the sort of thing I was always hearing about from the folks at the DTC. The president of the company, the supervisors, the superintendants, the secretaries, everyone knew me and gave me information on the goings-on I might find interesting. They did this because they knew I was excited.

As the '60s gave way to the '70s, so too did the Denver Tramway Corporation find itself replaced by the Regional Transportation District. At first, Kenton tried to keep the same level of connection between himself and this new transit entity, but it proved too difficult. Things changed too quickly, and he was no longer allowed the same access as before. Security measures did not permit the same freedom of movement. That is not to say that he left his passion for Denver's transit behind. He merely became more selective.

On the last day of DTC operation before RTD took over, the folks at the Tramway office gave me boxes full of stuff. Just everything: transfer books, lists of bus serial numbers, time cards, more. Do you want to know where the Number 13 was on any particular day and time? I can tell you where and when, who was driving and more.

Everything he collected, all the notes he had taken, were stored in his basement. Kenton began the time-consuming process of going through it all. He made copies of many things, donating them to museums, libraries and other pertinent agencies. Eventually, he would become involved with the Colorado Railroad Museum, where he was archivist for six years. He helped them design the library, which, immediately upon opening, everyone knew was too small. Some of the old train cars on site currently serve as storage units for the vast amounts of paper and information the museum has yet to process, though you would not know this from the outside of the cars. Eventually, the museum intends to expand its library, for the vast quantity of information still to be stored, as well as for the next generation of transit enthusiasts who will do research there.

Kenton recalls, "I was two people for all those years: the schoolteacher during the day, the tramway enthusiast on weekends. I never really shared that life with my students, since I was a science teacher. They were different worlds."

Once the Denver Tramway Corporation went away, Kenton did not limit his work to papers and museums, however. He kept his ear to the rails of old, so to speak, and made some special journeys even under the auspices of RTD.

Sixteenth Street was Denver's main street for shopping. It was converted into the mall that it is today in 1982, but before that it was a regular street that had cars on it. Long ago, it had streetcars on it as well. I rode the last scheduled bus to operate on Sixteenth Street before it was closed to vehicular traffic and buses were gone forever. Another colleague and I figured out what the last bus would be, the final one, and a big group of us got together to ride it. The lady driving the bus had no idea she was the last bus. One of the staff at the car barn told her, before she left, that people would be joining her, taking pictures. On a route and a time of day that normally had two or three people, she had fifteen plus people pile on, and we stopped for pictures. She drove us along the street and went up to Berkeley, the Route 28 at that time, and then went to the car barn, and another era was over. No longer would regular buses work that street at all.

The 16th Street Mall shuttle, a free transit mode carrying folks from the Light Rail station behind Union Station to Civic Center and back now occupies the roadway once filled with streetcars, cars and, later on, numerous buses. The pedestrian mall is one of Denver's top attractions.

Kenton also helped a number of colleagues in the three-volume work known as *Denver's Street Railways*. These are the definitive works on the subject of Denver's streetcar history.

We put everything in there that we could because no one else is going to work to that level of detail. The Denver Tramway is getting farther and farther away. Though there are groups out there working on aspects of its legacy, like museums and the Platte Valley Trolley, they are mostly on the hardware end of things. I am working the paper end. There is a vast amount of

Today, the 16th Street Mall and mall shuttles occupy the former domain of the viaduct. The Barteldes-Hartig Building, like the Morey Mercantile to its left in the picture, still bears marks of its connection to the viaduct.

information there, but going through it has to be a passion. It is not a career. There is no money in writing books on the tramways.

Kenton keeps finding things, and as a local expert, people frequently send him things that they find in their own possessions. One letter explained why Kenton was receiving some pictures unsolicited: "I found these pictures from a trip we took to Denver in the '40s, and here we are on the streetcar. I thought you might like to have them for the museum." One such picture showed the elusive Birch Street Loop, an example of which they had previously been unable to find. Too late for the book, but good to have for the future.

Later, when the Regional Transportation District began discussing the idea of putting in Light Rail, Kenton was glad. As someone who has studied public transit all his life—not just in Denver but all over the world—he knows that the general public has a very limited understanding of the true impact and the true limitations of this public service. As a government agency, for example, Amtrak is restricted from donating money to politicians. As such, it does not get the support that many other organizations get because they pay for their representation through lobbyists and donations. The United States Postal Service, Kenton continued, is criticized by many in comparison to private delivery operators. If those popular companies were required to deliver every piece of mail to even the remotest addresses in the nation, not just the popular routes, for one price, they too would find their profitability diminished. Public transit within metropolitan areas is akin to the postal service and interstate trains. These services are offered with public subsidy for the public good. Not everyone can own a car, and public transit allows everyone to get to work or to places of recreation. Public transit levels the field for all in a city.

> When the first Light Rail corridor was built, I was told by all kinds of people that it would never catch on at all, that it would be a dinosaur that would just sit there, unused. Those people had no insight into the future, no vision. Even the president of the RTD board at that time wanted to get rid of the idea. I told everyone, however, that once the rail went in, people would find it convenient and desirable. Every community would want to have one. This is just what has happened, and I am glad that it has been the visionaries who have had the final say.

Some things in the returning face of transit hearken back to what came before, too. The new West Corridor, scheduled to open in April 2013, will even have a schedule like the old interurban that used to run the same tracks back in 1931.

Kenton helped to promote the first Light Rail trips and got to work with folks at RTD on the project and remains attentive of its workings today. He looks forward to the line being continued from Thirtieth and Downing to join the East Corridor to the airport, a logical connection that will render the system more user-friendly for more people.

During this interview, Kenton considered a hypothetical question: if the Denver Tramway Corporation had wanted to do so, could it have kept the streetcars beyond 1950 and into the modern era?

> The grim realities facing the streetcars at that time were insurmountable. In 1950 the system was in horrible shape from decades of heavy use and years of neglect. Tracks and trolleys were coming apart. The city could do buses, but they had nowhere near enough money to put back into the system. They had to do something that would work with the money they had; the

company had stockholders. Also, the time had passed when streetcars were acceptable or in fashion. At that time, with huge amounts of money pouring into roadways, the car had the advantage. Cars gave people freedom of route and of schedule. Additionally, they were an expression of prosperity and excitement for people then, a novelty unlike the commonplace conveyance they are today. Finally, the DTC could never have maintained it in the face of public disinterest. Without public support, the streetcar was doomed.

In the Atomic Age, people were looking to the cars. Streetcars were bumbling relics of a bygone era. Just consider Tomorrowland at the Disney Parks. Part of the popularity of this part of the Magic Kingdom, right from opening day, was its focus on the technologies and possibilities of the future.

Despite the belief that the streetcars were something of the past, rail-based transit is making a comeback in Denver today. When asked why, Kenton's assessment pointed out how different Denver is currently from the city it was in the 1950s.

You will never get everyone out of their cars. Denver is not set up that way. Still, Light Rail and heavy commuter rail have a place in modern transit packages. Once the West Corridor opens, you watch: it will be packed. People will say "We want that" and act to get it. Once you get it going, people will come to it. You know, once a Light Rail train has gone in, that it is not going to be moved somewhere else. So, it's a great inducement to employers to locate near a Light Rail stop. The employers know that their employees will be able to get to work: look at DaVita and everything else relocating in the Union Station Redevelopment Area. Once the Denver/Boulder one is up, it will be gang busters. The streetcars were great, but they had some disadvantages too. The Light Rail trains of today are not exactly like the old streetcars. They are much bigger, for one thing, and that makes a tremendous difference. You would need three streetcars to make one Light Rail train. So, that's three operators on streetcars to one Light Rail operator. The Streetcars had small seats, you could not do bicycles, there was no access for handicapped people. Streetcars could never have handled the crowds heading to the baseball game, to the theater downtown. Of course, there are many more people now, but still, one Light Rail train can hold several hundred people, whereas one streetcar could hold nothing like that amount.

As such an advocate for transit history, it is unfortunate that Kenton had not been on the scene in Denver a little sooner and at a slightly older age. Folks have frequently lamented that so few of the old streetcars were actually kept, for museums, as tourist draws or anything else. The few that *do* exist in Denver today have had troubled histories themselves, and they are the exceptions. The mindset of the city's population was not the same in the 1950s, however. Historic preservation, only recently an accepted idea in most of the United States, was not even on people's mental radar in the heady years at the beginning of the 1950s. Retaining streetcars, so hackneyed and humdrum, would have been seen as a foolish sentimentality. Had Kenton been there, though, perhaps his enthusiasm would have led to the understanding of just what was about to be lost.

As for Kenton himself, there are things yet to see. He lives not far from the Oak Station, on the West Corridor, and may find the historic Car Number 25 housed there one day, a stone's throw from his house, with its basement full of transit treasure. Eventually, those transit treasures will all be at the museum. Until then, papers must be gone through, categorized and put in the proper place. Kenton is the last of a dying breed.

As Kenton and some of his colleagues wrote in *Mile-High Trolleys*:

> For anyone who lived in Denver before 1950, the memory of the big yellow trolleys will last far longer than the buses that replaced them. True, the tram cars were noisy. They rocked and swayed and their clanging bells demanded a clear path in traffic with disdain for the cars and buses that foretold their impending doom. They did, however, provide a growing city with the means of transportation it vitally needed. Several generations found them the best way to go to work or, just as important, to the ball park, City Park, the zoo or Elitch Gardens—even to the mountains via the Golden interurban. What was more wonderful than a trolley ride aboard an open car on a hot summer evening, or what more dependable in winter's blizzard than the faithful streetcar?

The year 1950 is not that long ago in many ways, but it is long enough that the echoes of the streetcar grow fainter every day. The voices of those who remember them are slowly being lost to us as well, so we record them here for posterity. Perhaps even the great tramway historians of yesteryear would approve.

CHAPTER 3

OUR RETURN TICKET

The old saying, "The more things change, the more they stay the same," would be a good way to begin this chapter. In the book *Time and Again,* a young woman from the modern day visits New York of the 1880s. A small exchange from this work of fiction illustrates the starting point for the chapter:

> *We boarded a hansom cab, asking for the main post office.*
> *"Can you do it in half an hour?" I asked.*
> *"I don't know," he said, disgustedly, and clucked at his horse, snapping the reins. We pulled out into the street. "The way traffic is nowadays, it gets worse every day, you never know anymore. We'll try it; straight down Fifth to the square shouldn't be too bad yet, this time of day. Then over to Broadway, and miss the damned El; pardon me, ma'am."*
> *I was smiling; however different, New York wasn't really changed.*

During the 1800s, many American cities, from Schenectady to Pueblo and beyond, built major transit infrastructure in a great paroxysm of growth. Later, as we have already seen, this trend was reversed in almost as many cities. Some cities, citing the value of multi-modal transit, are putting some of it back. Today Denver is one of these cities in the midst of a renewed exploration of transit. The amount of rail we may build out, as currently planned, will likely never reach the extent that it knew under the streetcar, but the trend is still toward more transit options rather than fewer. In this chapter, we examine the intervening years between the removal of the streetcar in 1950 and today, the course ahead for transit in the city and those pieces left to us indicative of what was once a city and region-spanning network. These elements are more disparate than the cohesive, linear story of transit history portrayed in the first chapter. This fragmentation may well be indicative of how small the pieces are when compared to the task ahead and our memory of what was.

The 1950s saw the nation as a whole gleefully embracing car culture. Referred to as one of the "greatest public works projects in history," President Eisenhower signed into law a sweeping series of changes to how the nation got around. Ostensibly intended to maximize the mobility of the nation's armies in any periods of crisis, the Eisenhower Interstate System, as it would be known, would make the citizens of the United States the "most mobile country in the world." Scenic routes, such as Route 66, and former significant thoroughfares, like Denver's Colfax Avenue, would be bypassed by the interstates, and so travelers left those old routes behind as well.

Though the streetcar left daily life in Denver in 1950, public transit was still provided. People were using the buses and trolley coaches (buses powered by the overhead electric lines) but in gradually diminishing numbers. The prosperous 1950s saw more people buying automobiles and moving to the suburbs, where it was harder to provide adequate transit coverage. Houses located farther and farther from the urban core stretched an already heavily stressed transit model beyond its capacity to compensate. To complicate matters, the ever-increasing number of cars contributed to a mêlée in streets that had been designed for the transit patterns and densities of earlier times. Streetcars, horse-drawn carriages and early automobiles were already said to cause traffic headaches in the early 1900s. During the 1950s, the problem grew much worse, the buses and trolley coaches now sharing the roads with more and more cars. Denver's transit gurus tried what changes they could to counter the increasing congestion. One-way streets were introduced into downtown and some of the neighborhoods that fed into it. Traffic engineers envisioned an increase to the speed and efficiency of traffic flow. These changes, it was hoped, would encourage more people to return to the buses for the daily commutes.

Despite the DTC's efforts, however, ridership continued to decline. An increase in traffic speed and efficiency merely encouraged more people to drive. To save money, and owing to diminished usage, routes ran less frequently or not at all at night and on weekends. Some were removed altogether. The trend was not unique to Denver; many transit entities around

The Denver Gas and Electric Building, still brightly lit today, rises behind this streetcar heading northwest on Fifteenth Street. Note the two-way traffic discernible in this shot. Fifteenth Street, as with many downtown, would later be made into a one-way thoroughfare. This is a Broadway streetcar, coming down to the Loop before heading back to Broadway for its trip south to Englewood.

the nation were struggling during this time period to continue offering *any* type of transit. It became starkly apparent that the modern era would no longer sustain a historic paradigm: transit as a privately owned enterprise. The time for inclusion of transit in those services offered by the government toward the public good had arrived. In 1969, the state legislature created the Regional Transportation District (a special district for taxation purposes) with a plan of taking over transit operations. In 1971, the Denver Tramway Corporation ceased operations and sold its assets to the City and County of Denver, which operated bus service within the city and suburbs as Denver Metro Transit. Transit, once battleground for investors during the heady final decades of the 1800s, had now passed completely into the hands of the government. In 1974, with voter approval of a half-cent sales tax, the City and County of Denver sold its Denver Metro Transit to the Regional Transportation District. RTD, as it is usually known, was now the primary transit player on Denver's stage, covering a consolidated service area that spread across the metropolitan area.

By the time this picture was taken at the Englewood Loop, about 1948, the streetcars were sharing the roadways with an increasing number of automobiles, making the going slower for many who had depended on transit much of their lives. *EPL.*

Honoring the pioneering spirit of its predecessor, RTD began major overhauls to its function and philosophy. Changes were necessary in order to bring riders back. One of the most forward thinking was the transformation of Sixteenth Street into the 16th Street Mall. The street was closed to automobile traffic in 1982 and transformed into its current form, designed by architect I.M. Pei. With free shuttles operating along its length, the hope was to draw people back to downtown Denver to shop and for fun. Today, the 16th Street Mall is one of the most popular attractions in the city. One group of Korean students, having spent a month in Denver during an intensive English program, was asked to write about their favorite aspect of the city; all twenty-four wrote about the mall, with its abundance of shopping, dining and entertainment, bound together by the ease of movement offered by the shuttle.

One of the areas where streetcars had been completely deficient was in accessibility for the handicapped. RTD undertook a series of very dramatic changes, including buses with lifts, designed to allow access for all people. Services such as Access-a-Ride would later complement these accommodations.

RTD continued its program of innovation and improvement because, with continued population growth into the area, traffic was becoming a serious problem for the city. Additionally, Denver had become nationally famous for its pollution—the "brown cloud" hanging over the skyline—leading to health alerts. In *Light Rail and Heavy Politics*, author Jack McCroskey illustrates part of the basis for these issues:

> *During the three decades beginning in 1970, the number of vehicle-miles driven in the United States skyrocketed some 130 percent; during the same time period lane-miles rose only fifteen percent. [Thus], lane-miles grew almost nine times faster than road-mile capacity. Given such disparate growth rates no one should be surprised it's taking commuters longer and longer to travel to and from work.*

As the length and difficulty of commutes became longer and Denver's pollution grew thicker, RTD proposed the introduction of trains on certain key transit corridors, in an effort to diminish all these problems. McCroskey continues:

> *Discontent surfaced during public meetings about RTD selecting a 19th-century technology, which some critics viewed as hopelessly out of date. In the end the board [of RTD] went with thoroughly tested surface Light Rail, determined not to invent anything and, insofar as possible, to buy absolutely nothing that couldn't be taken directly off the shelf. The remaining question: Where to put it? A tough issue made more difficult by the need to start with a very short line inside an immense district. Sprawling over six counties and 2,300 square miles—many of them sparsely populated—RTD encompasses an enormous area by comparative standards. It's geographically three times as large as systems in either Phoenix or Orange County; twice as big as those serving Atlanta and Portland; one-and-a-half times the size of those in Washington, DC and New York City. And yet metro Denver's three-million population base is less than the base in these other cities.*

Within those 2,300 square miles lie multiple cities, such as Arvada, Lone Tree, Erie, Longmont, Littleton, portions of Highlands Ranch and Castle Rock and more. Multiple counties were also embraced, such as Jefferson, Adams, Arapahoe, Douglas, Boulder, Denver, Broomfield and parts of Weld County. Thirty-one mayors, in multiple jurisdictions, were all working together as part of one transit entity. RTD is charged with maintaining transit as well as generating improvements for a diverse set of cities, counties, people and needs. As we shall learn shortly from the staff at RTD, Denver's transit model is one of the nation's best examples of regional cooperation and consolidated government service. Some metropolitan regions deal with transit through the format of each city doing its own thing. When RTD chose to implement Light Rail services, this agreement across borders made possible something that could never be implemented as readily in many places owing to intercity, intergovernmental and inter-jurisdiction issues. Whether rivalries, squabbling or just a guileless lack of cooperation, RTD saw trains as a big component of the future and moved to make their existence a reality. As a consolidated, single-service special district, it was able to more easily achieve its goals across the metropolitan area.

The daunting task of returning rail-based transit to the vast RTD region, to continue improving and expanding the region's transit potential, did not meet with universal approbation, however. The most common rejoinder, and one that has been heard frequently in the research for this book, is that people should just buy a car. This glib response, that the only viable transit option is personal car ownership, demonstrates a lack of prior deliberation on the part of the person making that response. It does not take into consideration all the reasons someone would *not* wish or be unable to buy a car. Children under a certain age may not legally drive a car. The aged and infirm may also be legally restricted. Automobile operation is not an option for many handicapped individuals; in the United States, striving to offer access for all people, public transit fulfills a vital and honorable function. Lastly, there are those who may not be able to afford a car. Beyond these, there are those who may choose to live without a car or to commute from time to time for personal reasons, such as economic and environmental concerns, or perhaps simply to have a chance to get a little extra sleep on the way to work, thus participating in a community-wide effort at combating more sprawl through the use of trains. Light Rail changes habits and choices of where some people choose to live and can lead to fewer cars on the road as a result. For all these individuals and more, transit provides a critical link to the wider world. So, honoring its mission to provide transit for all people, RTD moved forward with improvements to its system. In 1994, in addition to the first high occupancy vehicle (HOV) lanes, the Central Corridor of today's Light Rail network was put into place, connecting the intersection of I25 and Broadway with that at Thirtieth Avenue and Downing Street. There were numerous detractors predicting that the Central Corridor would prove a costly failure.

The results, as we shall see, have proven quite the opposite. Before examining these steps forward, however, let us tackle a question concerning the past. In discussing Denver's current transit infrastructure with third and fourth graders on downtown tours, one of the questions that has come up on a number of occasions has been: "Why didn't they just keep the streetcars?" For children born in this century, the decisions of the 1950s and prior are separated from their own lives by an infinite and largely incomprehensible gulf. Explanations were offered on why this did not happen; the answers seemed to satisfy the children. All the same, part of the research for this project involved querying others whose expertise lies in transit, both as historical and modern offerings.

An interview was conducted with several members of RTD staff: Pauletta Tonilas, media contact for FasTracks; John Elias, RTD historian; and Kevin Flynn, RTD public information officer. One of the questions posed to these individuals was the same one that had come from the school children: "Could the Denver Tramway Corporation have sustained the streetcars beyond the 1950s if they had tried?" The answers received, echoed by Kenton Forrest and others, was that the streetcars could not have been maintained.

The RTD staff members agreed that in the face of general public disdain for a technology that was seen as antiquated, at the time, there was no viable option for sustaining the streetcars. Public involvement and support is almost always necessary to make such a thing work. Most American cities had removed or were removing their streetcar grids by the time Denver did so, which meant that the mechanical challenge of keeping it would have grown exponentially. What company would have made replacement parts? Where would the DTC have gotten new streetcars if the system had been retained beyond 1950? The reduced availability of companies producing these items nationally would have meant that the tramway would have had to have taken on more and more of the burden itself, even down to the construction of streetcars. This would have been a prohibitively grueling task.

The only places in the United States where such systems were kept either had the density to warrant it, such as in New York City, or found the system emblematic of their city itself. San Francisco's cable cars were an expression of the city's image and served as a tourist draw. In such cases, streetcars and similar systems had the power to stay beyond the impetus felt nationally. In Denver, though there were certainly those who held streetcars in high esteem and felt nostalgia for them, the metropolitan area itself was not defined *by the streetcars* in such a way that would have given them staying power. Without that association, and in the face of public pressure to modernize, the streetcars could not have kept to their tracks. Now, with an understanding that the gap between rail-based transit *then* and rail-based transit *now* was unavoidable, we continue our historic journey.

The original Light Rail line was paid for entirely out of money RTD had on hand (through fares and the tax base that supports its function), without an increase in taxation within the district. Despite public doubts, RTD felt that the time was right for rail to be reintroduced to Denver. There was much debate of where, precisely, the rail would go. The choice of route between the locations at I25 and Broadway and Thirtieth and Downing allowed for a minimum amount of removal within the built environment, while still linking the heavily traveled southern approach to Denver. To the north, the Thirtieth and Downing corridor, as it was originally intended, would eventually link downtown to the airport (at that time, plans were in the final stages to move the airport from Stapleton to its current location). The Central Corridor opened in 1994, and RTD's gamble was laid upon the table; Denver's commuters and fate would decide.

Ridership on the original Central Corridor far exceeded RTD's expectations from the first day. Emboldened by its success, RTD continued the expansion of its rail network, opening the Southwest Corridor in 2000 and the Central Platte Valley extension in 2002. With these lines, commuters could use parking facilities and kiss-and-rides (pull outs near transit stations where a spouse who is staying home may drop off the spouse who is commuting to work; after the kiss good-bye, the commuter takes the train to work, and the stay-at-home spouse drives back to the family's residence). These offerings allow people to leave their cars behind for the commute into downtown Denver. Beyond the daily commute, the lines also took people to enjoy the entertainment venues in downtown. Downtown Denver and the area immediately adjacent offer stadiums for basketball, hockey, baseball and football. The famous Elitch Gardens Amusement Park relocated to downtown Denver, opening in 1995. The Denver Center for the Performing Arts—the largest theatrical venue in the country under one roof—numerous restaurants, bars, shopping and more all called people into the city's vibrant downtown, a downtown made all the more successful by offering multiple ways to get there.

This has been key to Denver's success: options. Multi-modal transit means having more than one way of getting around a city, with bike paths and pedestrian malls, buses, shuttles, trains and, of course, automobile access. RTD's goal was not to get rid of the car. Rather, RTD sought to create a city based on choices. "The point of transit is not to force people to stop driving," said Pauletta Tonilas. "The point of transit is to give people choices." If a person wants to drive, that person may drive. Reaching downtown via automobile allows for maximum freedom in schedule and location but puts one directly in the face of traffic and high parking costs. For those who wish to avoid the crushing traffic after the plays and games are done, Light Rail offers an alternative. This alternative, however, still has some bumps to traverse.

One of the most enduring difficulties that RTD has had to face has been the opinions held on to concerning transit, especially among the generation that came of age when automobiles were sweeping the nation. One of the people interviewed in Chapter Two, Clarence, had mixed feelings about the streetcars of his youth. His opinions about the Light Rail, however, are not so kind:

> *I've ridden the Light Rail once, and it was horrible. We live near Yale and I225 now. We took the grandkids to a baseball game downtown, at Coors Field. Once we got on, at the Nine Mile Station, it took us forty-five minutes to get to our final stop, and then we had to hire a pedicab to get us to the stadium. What a waste of time. If we had driven, the whole journey would have taken us fifteen minutes from leaving home to getting to the game. We would have had to have paid for parking, but we paid for the tickets on the train as it was, so the real cost was the time. I think transit in general is an enormous waste of money, a distraction from what we should be doing with our taxes. I guess it's ok if you have lots of spare time, but if you're trying to get someplace in a hurry, I just wouldn't take it. I hope the line out to the airport won't have to stop all the time; I would take the line to the airport if it didn't make lots of stops.*

Clarence's statement that the trip from Yale and I225 to Coors Field would have taken fifteen minutes, door to door, is a perfect example of the difficulties facing RTD today in changing public opinion. The most efficient route, suggested by an online mapping website, would have taken Clarence and his family, by car, north along I225, then westward along I70, than along I25 south and into downtown, a distance of eighteen miles lasting, at optimal speeds and with no traffic, twenty-four minutes. This is not a number particularly higher than the fifteen minutes Clarence asserted, but this amount of time fails to take into account the unpleasant fact that one does not go to athletic events alone: a large number of other people will *also* be going, which means the area around the stadium will be congested.

Denver's highways do not always allow maximum speeds to be achieved or maintained. In the end, whether the amount of time traveling via Light Rail is really consistently greater than that offered by a car at critical periods of high traffic on highways and on downtown Denver streets, the point is that many people *believe* it to be so. That *belief* has shown great longevity. Not everyone believes thusly, however. For many, even though time on a bus or train might be longer, it offers compensatory benefits, such as freedom to read, watch programs on mobile devices and even sleep. These, we hope, are not activities taken by those at the wheel of an automobile. So, RTD's journey was never just about updating the choices we have in travel but also about improving how we view the idea of travel itself. Washington, D.C., offered support in Denver's efforts concerning mass transit.

The federal government, in an effort to promote diversified transit packages, has given RTD grants to further expand its multi-modal system. One of these improvements, the Southeast Corridor, opened in 2006, having been constructed as an integral aspect of the Colorado Department of Transportation's I25 expansion and remediation project, known colloquially as T-Rex. The federal government supported T-Rex in large part owing to its inclusion of the Light Rail corridor. Federal and district-wide governmental support of continued expansion was something that the public encouraged through its primary method of expression: its votes. In 2004, the voters of the region approved a sales tax increase to fund FasTracks, a landmark rapid transit expansion that would include expanded Light Rail, (powered by overhead electric wires just like the original streetcars), heavy commuter rail, bus rapid transit lanes and more. It was a strong representation of support from the citizens, a roar of approval. With full steam ahead, to borrow a nautical phrase, the immediate prospects for RTD and its constituents appeared high.

At this point, however, economic woes within the nation slowed the pace of FasTracks' implementation. Costs for all basic materials, including cement, steel, fuel and more, went up while sales tax revenue went down. The original timeline for the completion of all elements of FasTracks had been 2015; this had to be modified. Though slowed, RTD did not stop. In 2011, the federal government awarded RTD a one-billion-dollar grant, the fourth grant RTD had received and its largest, to fund the heavy commuter rail line to the airport (the East Corridor) and the lines to the northwest suburbs. Throughout all of it, the staff at RTD has shown remarkable tenacity and vision, creating new tools to get things done even in times of economic hardship. These laudable traits are ones that have not escaped notice by other transit agencies around the nation. Pauletta Tonilas, who provides information to the public as well as fellow organizations within the world of transit, explained:

> *City and transit planners come to study us all the time. We just had visitors from Detroit coming to see how we are doing public-private partnerships. People want to know how we, as a transit agency, were able to collaborate with a governmental agency, the CDOT* [Colorado Department of Transportation] *in order to build out T-Rex. How do we get different city and county governments to participate, and how, during a time of economic recession, are we still able to move forward? These are the areas where people from around the United States and even other countries look to us for answers.*

When it comes to transit, Denver is setting the example that others are trying to emulate. One of the most successful methods RTD has implemented is its public-private partnerships. Lacking the funding to tackle the I225 rail line presently, RTD had shelved the project for the time being. RTD was approached by Kiewit, a company based out of Omaha. Offering a number of services, including construction of transportation infrastructure, Kiewit asserted it could have the entire line built out and opened to the public, connecting the Nine-Mile Station along I225, then through the Fitzsimons Campus to the East Corridor, by 2016. Once evaluated, the proposal was found to hold merit, so the line is moving forward. Kiewit will front the costs of the line, which RTD will pay back later, eventually acquiring full ownership of the line and associated structures. The city wins, commuters win, Kiewit's employees have work to do and RTD will get to mark another box as completed. All thirty-one mayors in the area approved of RTD's plans to move forward with FasTracks, voting unanimously during a Metro Mayors Caucus. It was partly that unified vision that got FasTracks moving in the first place. Creative solutions, such as this public-private partnership with Kiewit, have kept FasTracks moving, despite unforeseen hindrances. To borrow a slight pun, rail has shown its mettle.

John Elias explained the reasons behind the continued progress, despite complications delaying the original design:

> *From the time the streetcar went away until when we opened the first line in 1994, there were many people who thought rail would never be a success. They thought no one would ride it if we DID build new rail. All our lines*

have far exceeded expectations; even on opening day they've been far beyond the projections. People DO love the trains and they DO take the trains, and they want more and more of them. After doing without a rail operation for that many years, people have really embraced it and are using it. They realize how easy it is. Transit brings you back time in your day, because there are things you can't do as you're driving that you CAN do in transit, like read or even sleep.

Before leaving behind this perusal of RTD's methods, one helpful tool put into work by the folks at RTD should be examined. In an effort to build smartly and make every dollar stretch as far as possible, RTD has kept assiduous notes on all it has learned so that these lessons may be applied to future projects. In this way, mistakes will not be made twice, and methods that have proven reliable may be applied again without having to be relearned. The RTD website features a section from past projects called Lessons Learned. These are referred to continually at RTD and are available to the public.

Kevin Flynn brought up a lesson learned during the 1960s and 1970s in Denver that is being applied today: having the government offer transit was the best choice then, and it is the best choice now.

Public transit no longer works when provided by the private sector. Mass transit has to serve all parts of the participating metropolitan area, even the areas that do not earn a profit. The post office has to deliver to everyone—across the nation and in remote areas—for the same fixed rate, where FedEx and similar companies may make a big profit from just doing the lucrative routes. Transit follows the same basic principles.

By having the government step in to provide transit, everyone is served and everyone has access. Transit provided by small companies owned and directed by private individuals worked when streetcars and the like were the only option. In a time of greater competition and variety, private companies cannot generally cover the costs. So, transit is subsidized by the public for the public good, as many services are, such as parks, museums and schools. While the idea of subsidizing something may be anathema to many, doing so does not come without many gains.

Rail transit provides great economic return as well. A train, with one operator at the helm, can carry up to five hundred passengers, a number a bus could not hope to achieve. With trains running every fifteen minutes throughout much of the day, the potential for moving people in an efficient and comfortable manner is enormous. This reduces the amount of traffic and the amount of pollution, as well as the amount of consternation experienced by those suffering from either. Further, Light Rail has also been found to spur real estate development, just as streetcars did in the 1800s. Time and again in Denver, it has been demonstrated that people follow the rail. When the Southeast Corridor stops were announced, the real estate by those stops became much sought after by those who wanted to be close to transit options. Today's Union Station redevelopment has been successful owing to the same conclusion. People living by transit have choices. If they want to drive, they drive. If they want to take the train, this is also available to them. In the winter, there are even times when trains offer some perks. Trains, not subject to the vicissitudes of weather, allow people to get to work dependably without worrying about dangerous roads and the fear of accidents. Employers, especially, like knowing that their workers will be able to reach them. This has been one of the reasons for several high-profile companies locating in the Union Station redevelopment area.

By embracing transit, the people of Denver have earned many points of pride. Denver is a city admired by others around the nation for its energetic downtown, which has experienced a surge in population, according to the latest census figures. Beyond those who live in downtown are the many who come in from the neighborhoods and suburbs to enjoy what downtown has to offer. For all of it, transit has been integral. Denver's future is very bright, and the transit choices that it is making today will make further accomplishments in this century all the easier to achieve.

We have now made our way through the entire transit history of the Denver metropolitan region, reaching the modern day, where the year 2012 is waning. Even with all this, there will be many changes that await us. Before we conclude, however, we set aside considerations of the glittering future for a moment and make one more nod to the past. Whatever the streetcar was—an archaic transit mode unmourned or a tragic loss in a city rushing heedlessly forward—it is still with us today in many ways. Here and there, pieces of it may be found poking up through the ashes of time. We list them here and chronicle their journeys so that those readers who wish to touch some of our streetcar history rather than merely read about it may do so.

For train aficionados, the region and state offer a number of options, such as the Cumbres and Toltec Scenic Railroad (a remnant of the state's narrow gauge railroad system). In Golden, visitors may enjoy the Colorado Railroad Museum, the current and eventual repository for much of Kenton Forrest's collection of artifacts as well as his wisdom. In Denver, the Forney

Museum of Transportation also provides information and objects from our transit past. Even the History Colorado Center, home of the Colorado Historical Society, has gotten in on the act: visitors may drive a mockup of an antique car across the plains of eastern Colorado. All these institutions, from functioning trains to museums, provide a link between the modern day and how we got around before.

The Denver Tramway Heritage Society works to preserve streetcar history specifically. It is composed of volunteers only, men and women who have gotten together to keep streetcars alive for future generations to take pleasure in, as previous generations did. Three of the volunteers—Bruce Vincent, Darrell Arndt and Thomas Peyton—were interviewed concerning the society's function.

The primary activity pursued by the society is the operation of the Platte Valley Trolley. Running along the South Platte River near the old Platte Street power plant (built in 1901, it is itself a remnant of the Denver Tramway Company's function), the trolley carries around twenty thousand people every year, from almost every state and many countries. This is an activity center for the city, especially liked by kids. The trolley is being integrated into the offerings of the Confluence Park area and will continue to serve as a viable tourist draw. The southern part of the track may even be extended. The folks at the Denver Tramway Heritage Society are working with the city to determine where this extension would best serve the community. One prospect is having the trolley continue to the Decatur Station (a station on the West Corridor, slated to open April 2013). As pointed out in both Chapters One and Three, rail expansion did not and does not come without the possibility of dissent. A Light Rail line will soon serve this part of Denver, and wherever the rail goes, so goes development. The neighborhood to the south of the Decatur Station, Sun Valley, is the poorest in the city. The city has great plans for improvement to it, owing to the newfound draw of the Light Rail. Some parties, however, involved with Sun Valley's redevelopment have stated they do not want the Platte Valley Trolley in their neighborhood.

"The companies developing the big condos there are worried that it will detract from their properties' values," Darrell Arndt expounded. "So, we might end up extending into the Lower Colfax area, contributing to the revitalization there. This would make Lower Colfax a new, miniature Main Street, involving the city, the trolley and the Stadium District." Darrell and his colleagues feel that the presence of the Platte Valley Trolley would be a boon to any neighborhood, but this belief is not shared by everyone. Clearly, some issues remain contentious, no matter how many years pass.

Built in 1901 by the Denver Tramway Company to provide power for its many streetcars, the Platte Street Power Plant has undergone a number of changes in use. It served as the Forney Museum of Transportation for a while and is today the local flagship of REI.

Another very significant project undertaken by the folks at the Denver Tramway Heritage Society and the Rocky Mountain Railroad Club has been the restoration of Car Number 25. This vehicle used to run on the Denver and Intermountain Railroad, serving Route 84 to Golden. Work on the car itself has been largely concluded. The city of Lakewood, owners of the interurban car, intends to build a carhouse near the Oak Street Station (on the West Corridor). This will serve to house the vehicle, making it available to the public. Though it is currently not independently mobile, the folks in Lakewood hope to offer short runs on Number 25 at some point in the future, a suburban equivalent of the rides presently available on the Platte Valley Trolley. The folks at the Denver Tramway Heritage Society, intimately connected to the effect transit has on a community, were very upbeat about Denver's future owing to the steps it is making today concerning transit.

Having been refurbished by the Denver Tramway Heritage Society and the Rocky Mountain Railroad Club, Car Number 25 serves as a vital link to the city's transit past. Car Number 25 may one day take visitors on short excursions from its future home at the Oak Street Station. *Lakewood Heritage Center.*

The Platte Valley Trolley, with the rides of Elitch's in the background, takes rail fans along the South Platte River for a taste of Denver's streetcar past. The trolley is one of the main efforts of the Denver Tramway Heritage Society. *DTHS.*

People need to remember that FasTracks is not for the next five or ten years, it's for the next fifty to one hundred years. The city is just going to continue to grow. Los Angeles was once the same size as Denver. In fifty years, the trains will be even more used than they are now. Younger generations are into transit, they're into living downtown where they don't need cars, where they can get around using transit. There will be more concentrated development around transit options so people may take advantage of what we are building today.

To clarify, this is known as Transit Oriented Development (TOD) and is a national trend. In a study put out by the Center for Transit-Oriented Development in 2004, research demonstrated that "demand for higher-density housing in transit zones could far outstrip the supply of this kind of housing. All the regions [in the United States] that are expanding their transit systems have the potential for high rates of growth in housing demand, especially regions like Denver, Salt Lake City and Seattle, which have expanding systems and high rates of population growth. Indeed, many of these regions with newer systems could accommodate from a quarter to a third of all household growth in transit zones."

On the other side of the metropolitan area is Trailer Number 610. As a trailer, it had no motor. It would have been attached to a streetcar to add capacity during times of need, such as rush hour traffic. The car was constructed by the Woeber Company for the Denver Tramway Company in 1913, one of the last twenty-six cars built for them by that company. Number 610 served on Colfax during peak rush hours from 1914 until 1932. Retired from service, the vehicle ended up following an unusual course. Most streetcars and trailers, once removed from the fleet, would be scrapped or quite literally put out to pasture, where they would slowly decay. Trailer Number 610, however, was bought by Dr. Edwin Perrott in 1950. He put the trailer on his property in Aurora and built his house around it. Removing many of the interior features, Dr. Perrott used it as his bedroom and office. After Dr. Perrott's death, the vehicle was donated to the Aurora History Museum by his heirs. Dr. Perrott had not maintained the vehicle historically; he had cut three doors into one side and removed interior seating, but the frame was sound. The restoration of the vehicle took over 4,300 hours, involved sixteen volunteers and an estimated $175,000 from cash and in-kind donations. Eventually, the Aurora History Museum will build an addition to its facility to house the trailer. For now, it remains hidden away from the public. Once Car

Dr. Perrott's former bedroom and office has been refurbished by hard-working and enthusiastic volunteers at the Aurora History Museum. Though not yet available for public inspection, the restored streetcar will one day be given its own area within the expanded museum.

Car 610, long buried within a man's house, has today been given a fresh coat of paint and a new lease on a historic future.

Number 25 and Trailer Number 610 reach their final homes, however, members of the public will once again be able to stand in vehicles that last saw service in the 1950s.

There are some additional success stories to add to these, signs of projects to come. At the RTD offices near Ringsby Court and Thirty-first Street, in Denver, two streetcar vehicles and some of the old buses lie moldering in a garage. Attacked by time as well as by raccoons, the trailers have not fared well. RTD must tear the building down to create space for the transit lines leaving downtown Denver for points north and east, which means the vehicles must have new homes. In the autumn of 2012, the vehicles were offered for purchase. A deal was struck, and they will soon go to a transit museum in Colorado Springs, where they will be refurbished and put on display. Colorado Springs also has a rich transit history, and these preserved vehicles will help in educating the public.

For those of you who wish to ride a vehicle from the streetcar era, hear the clang of the bell and maybe even feel the pinch of a wicker seat, these are some of the local possibilities. Especially for the generations of children who never knew the world of streetcars, it is a powerful way to make a connection to a once-flourishing aspect of our past. Beyond these remnants, there are other less obvious signs of the streetcar. These marks are not always readily associated with streetcars, but the connections are there all the same. Through careful observation, you too may find them and know them for what they are. Some of them are listed here for your further exploration.

At the corner of the 16th Street Mall and Wynkoop are two buildings, the Barteldes-Hartig Building and the Morey Mercantile, the latter now the home for the Tattered Cover Bookstore. The bookstore has entrances on both the Wynkoop and Sixteenth Street sides of the building. One accesses the Barteldes-Hartig Building from Wynkoop. Those entering the Tattered Cover from the 16th Street Mall side generally do so completely ignorant to the streetcar history over their heads. Above them, on the next level of both the Morey Mercantile and the Barteldes-Hartig Buildings, are grander entrances. This might cause some anxiety for those who notice the incongruity today. Surely using those doors would lead to a painful fall to the pavement below. The layout of the street was not always the same, however. Earlier, in Chapter One, the viaducts of downtown Denver were mentioned. Once numerous, they carried pedestrians, private vehicles and streetcars up and over the dangerous and delaying Union Station Train Yard or other impediments. Eventually, when the Union Station area had

Though its exterior has been vandalized by humans and its interior has been the shredding ground of rodents, this old streetcar will be removed from an RTD storage facility and given new life in Colorado Springs.

A streetcar rests by an old trolley coach, still showing the flexible arms that would have connected it to its overhead power source. Muted by time and isolation, they nevertheless tell a story about an energetic city and its extensive transit system.

become moribund and in an effort to make Lower Downtown (or LoDo, as it is now known) more appealing, these viaducts were removed. The Sixteenth Street Viaduct began at Wazee and rose at a steep grade to pass over Wynkoop and the train yards beyond. The Morey and Barteldes Buildings, on either side, would have been accessible via walkways from the viaduct. The doorways bore embellishments worthy of the businesses within, decorative features that were left quite literally up in the air when the viaduct was removed.

Most people driving around Denver will note differences in the size of some streets apparent to even the most casual observer. Some of this is owing to certain roads having a special designation, such as being state or national highways. Others owe their size to the fact that they used to have streetcars. Twenty-fifth and Twenty-eighth Avenues, in the Whittier neighborhood, are wider than the roadways on either side. Bannock southbound from Sixth Avenue is wider than Cherokee or Acoma on either side, until it reaches First Avenue, where it diminishes in size. The

Denver General Hospital is just outside the picture to the left and farther down the street in this view eastward along Sixth Avenue.

streetcar turned at that point, continuing southbound on Cherokee. Thus, a wider Bannock was no longer necessary. These wider streets are not the mere caprice of the neighborhood's developer or the city; they are often indications of a streetcar route, even though the streetcars themselves are gone and the rails have sometimes been paved over completely rather than removed.

Before concluding, we come to one of the most powerful legacies left behind by the streetcar today, an inheritance that has greatly contributed to Denver's vigor. In Chapter One, the effect that streetcars had on neighborhoods was discussed, especially as it pertains to islands of retail within residential neighborhoods. This neighborhood format was the norm for years in cities throughout the United States. The unrestrained expansion of the suburbs after World War II, following the model of Levittown, New York, changed the dynamic markedly. These communities were not set up with walking in mind. People were intended to drive to most destinations. Zoning laws, upheld by the Supreme Court in 1926 as being among the repertoire of legal options available to a city, also played a part. Mixed-use developments were gradually diminished.

People were expected to live *here*, shop *here* and work *here*, and the uses were separated by distances that required driving. Zoning regulations of the 1950s and the success of residential developments typical of those in the suburbs solidified the control of the automobile, and the trend continued. Throughout Denver, many of these islands of retail function were lost or torn down in favor of their new templates. Not all were lost, however. Once these neighborhoods returned to favor, these islands of retail function would serve as the nuclei of some of the most vibrant success stories in the revitalization of those neighborhoods.

After World War II, many people wanted to live in the suburbs, where everything was bright, shiny and new, decked out with the latest technologies and fully embodying the prosperity of the time. Many of the residents of Denver's historic neighborhoods, such as Curtis Park, Five Points, Highlands, Harman and Baker, left for these beacons on the horizon. Property values plummeted in the interior of the city. Without investment from the residents, there was often no economic inducement to tear down the structures of old, unless something large was planned. (For example, the area south of Harman, a former dump, was remade into the Cherry Creek Shopping Center, deriving its name from the adjacent creek. The development would later lend its name to the neighborhood as a whole. The Number 4 streetcar once ran along Second and Third Avenues in Cherry Creek North.) Houses and businesses in these older and somewhat forgotten neighborhoods and others were largely ignored until the idea of historic preservation could take root in Denver and have enough time to bloom.

Urban pioneers realized that most of these neighborhoods had grand old Victorian homes, many of them dating back to the 1800s. Some of the homes had been severely neglected, true, but that neglect led to many of them selling for next to nothing. Those people able to spend the money on household renovation would thus find themselves in possession of a historic structure within a negligible distance from downtown Denver. This was a very tempting combination for many people, especially in an era when commutes were growing longer and more odious. One of the other carrots on a stick was those original islands of retail. These businesses could be remade as readily as the houses, becoming restaurants, doggy bath establishments, yoga studios, art galleries and more. As the neighborhoods were reinvigorated, the restaurants were themselves reborn, thus further enhancing the neighborhoods, a circle of continuing benefit. As Pauletta Tonilas, at RTD, pointed out: everything old is new again. Today, these once neglected areas have become some of

Taken about 1910 at the intersection of Broadway and Hampden (then known as Sheridan), this photograph illustrates the density of businesses that would often spring up around streetcar stops. These islands of retail would serve as the nuclei of some of Denver's most sought-after neighborhoods today. *EPL.*

Former streetcar intersections, like this one at South Pearl and Louisiana, retain some of the business function that illustrates their transit past. These retail hubs within neighborhoods have proven quite popular for a generation of modern Denverites less interested in driving everywhere.

the most sought-after real estate in the city. Though the streetcars are long gone, the islands of retail they left behind are still lending potency to the neighborhoods they call home. Thirty-second and Lowell, Thirty-second and Zuni, South Pearl, South Gaylord, Forty-fourth and Tennyson, First and Broadway and more serve as examples that stand out for their history, friendliness to walkers and enhanced feeling of community. More than perhaps anything else left behind by the streetcar, this is the aspect most valuable to us today.

Concluding the history of the streetcar is not really possible, for it is still being written around us. The Denver Tramway Company that was once such a powerful force for development in Denver now manifests as the Regional Transportation District, still pursuing development for the public good. Though not streetcars precisely, their modern equivalents, the Light Rail trains, carry people across many miles of track. People still go to work, play and meet each other using transit in Denver, and this network of rails will only continue to expand. This can only benefit everyone involved. Though much of the information related in this book has been reported as mere history, the tone is unabashedly pro-transit, the same tone that was struck in the three-volume definitive work on our transit past, *Denver's Street Railways*. There is no apology to be made for this clear preference for transit. Although population growth in the United States—and the world at large—may one day level out or even diminish, that point does not lie in our immediate future. Buying more cars, building more roads and expanding the roads we have…these are not viable options for Denver. Traffic is already problematic for many; how would more cars rectify that? We already have numerous roads in a metropolitan area stretching across vast distances. From Golden in the west to the eastern boundary of Aurora is a distance of more than forty miles. The expanse of cityscape covering the Front Range in the opposite direction is even bigger. If we build wider and wider roads, where will we live? How much soil must be paved over for us ALL to be able to drive?

When FasTracks is done, it will reach a vast area, serving millions of people. New lines will include the Gold Line to Arvada; the North Metro Line to Commerce City, Thornton, Northglenn and beyond; the Northwest Line to Boulder and Longmont; extensions on existing lines; bus-rapid-transit lanes; and more. It will not happen overnight, but neither did Denver's first efforts in rail-based transit, which stretched across eighty years. The point of it all is to give people choices, and who doesn't like to have choices? For Denver, the menu of choices is getting bigger. This is a good thing.

Here and there, signs of the streetcars remain with us. This was part of
the Union Station Loop. From here to the Sixteenth Street Viaduct you
could take yourself up the stairs to get on the streetcar and go north or in
reverse to go TO the train station. This piece of rail, sticking up through
the pavement on Wynkoop just north of Fifteenth Street, reminds us of
what we have lost and how the legacy of the streetcars can still pop up in
the most surprising places!

Denver's streetcar history is not unique. Most every city of size in the
United States had streetcars. What sets Denver apart are the efforts we
are taking to preserve our streetcar history and the choices we are making
to bring back the best parts of what was lost. The *clang-clang* of the bell is
returning. Can you hear it calling? Let's enjoy the ride together.

BIBLIOGRAPHY

Betteman, Ollo L. *The Good Old Days—They Were Terrible!* New York: Random House, 1974.

Breck, Allen duPont. *William Gray Evans 1855–1924*. Denver, CO: Allan Swallow Publisher, 1964.

Bryson, Bill. *At Home*. London: Doubleday, 2010.

Cafky, Morris, E.J. Haley and Don Robertson. *Denver's Street Railways, Volume One*. Denver, CO: Sundance Publications Ltd., 1999.

Cafky, W. Morris, and Don Robertson. *Denver's Street Railways, Volume 2*. Denver, CO: Sundance Publications, Ltd., 2004.

Curtis Park: Denver's Oldest Neighborhood. Denver, CO: Historic Denver, Inc., 2002.

Erbsen, Wayne. *Manners and Morals of Victorian America*. Charlotte, NC: Native Ground Books and Music, 2009.

Feitz, Leland. *Colorado Trolleys*. Denver, CO: Golden Bell Press, 1971.

Finney, Jack. *Time and Again*. New York: Simon and Schuster Inc., 1970.

Fletcher, Ken. *Centennial State Trolleys: The Life and Times of Colorado's Streetcars*. Boulder, CO: Johnson Printing Company, 1995.

———. *A Mile High and Three Feet Six Wide*. Aurora, CO: Mountain West Enterprises, 1993.

Forrest, Kenton, and Don Robertson. *Denver's Street Railways, Volume 3*. Golden: Colorado Railroad Museum, 2010.

Forrest, Kenton, William Jones, Gene McKeever and F. Hol Wagner. *Mile-High Trolleys*. Denver, CO: Intermountain Chapter, National Railway Historical Society, Inc., 1975.

Griffith, Stanwood. *Denver Tramways*. New York: Electric Railroaders' Association, Inc., 1961.

Grinstead, Leigh A. *Molly Brown's Capitol Hill Neighborhood*. Denver, CO: Historic Denver, Inc., 1997.

Hansen, William J., and Thomas J. Noel. *The Montclair Neighborhood*. Denver, CO: Historic Denver, Inc., 1999.

Heilbroner, Robert L. *The Economic Transformation of America: 1600 to the Present*. New York: Harcourt Brace Jovanovich, Publishers, 1984.

Hidden in Plain Sight; Capturing the Demand for Housing Near Transit. Berkeley, CA: Center for Transit-Oriented Development, 2004.

Jeurink, Mary Louise. *The Buster Book*. Denver, CO: self-published, 2001.

McCroskey, Jack. *Light Rail and Heavy Politics*. Denver, CO: Tenlie Publishing, 2003.

Millhiser, Marlys. *The Mirror*. Boulder, CO: Rue Morgue Press, 1978.

Noel, Thomas J. *Growing through History with Colorado*. Denver: Colorado National Banks and the Colorado Studies Center, 1987.

———. *Mile High City*. Denver, CO: Heritage Media Corporation, 1997.

Paglia, Michael, Rodd L. Wheaton and Diane Wray. *Denver: The Modern City*. Denver, CO: Historic Denver, Inc., 1999.

Raughton, Jim L. *Whittier Neighborhood and San Rafael Historic District*. Denver, CO: Historic Denver, Inc., 2004.

Simmons, Laurie, and Thomas H. *East Colfax Avenue*. Denver, CO: Historic Denver, Inc., 2007.

Snow, Shawn M. *Denver's City Park and Whittier Neighborhoods*. Charleston, SC: Arcadia Publishing, 2009.

So, Frank S. *The Practice of Local Government Planning*. Washington, D.C.: International City Management Association, 1988.

West, William Allen. *Curtis Park, a Denver Neighborhood*. Boulder: Colorado Associated University Press, 1980.

Widmann, Nancy L. *Washington Park*. Denver, CO: Historic Denver, Inc., 2007.

INDEX

U

Union Pacific 15
University of Denver 29, 46, 67, 77
University Park Railway and Electric
    Company 30

V

Valverde 20
von Richtofen, Baron 20

W

Walker, John Brisbane 30
Whittier 18, 131, 138
Woeber Brothers Carriage Company
  Woeber Brothers 19

ABOUT THE AUTHOR

Kevin Pharris reached Denver relatively late in life, owing to his being a military brat. Once settled in Denver, he found the history, the dichotomy of historic versus modern and the vitality of the city's drive toward the future very compelling. These elements beguiled him out of the world of English as a Second Language teaching and into that of history as a profession. Living in one of the city's first streetcar suburbs, the Whittier neighborhood, he has chosen to remain carless. For more than seventeen years, he has walked, ridden his bike, taken the train or bus and (to be entirely fair) occasionally had rides from friends in order to get here and there. Being carless turned him on to the transit history of the city. Denver's bold move to restore multimodal transit to the area inspired him to examine a present and future that serve as complements to the past. He'll remain carless for now, thrilled to ride the rails into the future along with the rest of those lucky few who call Denver home.

Visit us at
www.historypress.net